UFC'S ULTIMATE
WARRIORS
T(THE)P 10

JEREMY WALL

Published by ECW PRESS
2120 Queen St. East, Suite 200, Toronto, Ontario, Canada M4E 1E2

NATIONAL LIBRARY AND ARCHIVES CANADA CATALOGUING IN PUBLICATION DATA

Wall, Jeremy, 1984–
UFC's Ultimate Warriors: The Top 10 / Jeremy Wall.
ISBN 1–55022–691–6
1. Martial artists—Biography. I. Title.
GV1111.W34 2005   796.8'092'2   C2004-907053-3

Copyediting and production: Emma McKay
Design and typesetting: Guylaine Régimbald—www.solo-d.ca
Cover photo courtesy of Frank Shamrock
Back cover photos: Severn by April Pishna; Shamrock/Ortiz by Stephen Quadros
Printing: Transcontinental

This book is set in DTL Caspari.

The publication of UFC's *Ultimate Warriors: The Top 10* has been generously
supported by the Canada Council, the Ontario Arts Council, and the Government
of Canada through the Book Publishing Industry Development Program. Canada

DISTRIBUTION

CANADA: Jaguar Book Group, 100 Armstrong Avenue, Georgetown,
        Ontario, L7G 5S4

UNITED STATES: Independent Publishers Group, 814 North Franklin Street,
        Chicago, Illinois, 60610

EUROPE: Turnaround Publisher Services, Unit 3, Olympia Trading Estate,
        Coburg Road, Wood Green, London N22 6T2

AUSTRALIA AND NEW ZEALAND: Wakefield Press, 1 The Parade West (Box 2066),
        Kent Town, South Australia, 5071

ECW PRESS
ecwpress.com

This book is dedicated to my mother.

Table of Contents

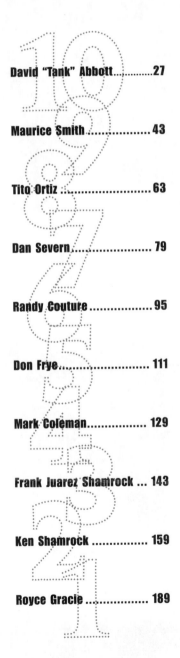

Acknowledgments

I want to thank the following people, all of whom contributed to this project and have helped me along the way. I made this list in no particular order. If you're not on here, and you think you should be, then I'm sorry I hurt your feelings, but I'm sure you'll get over it.

Dale Wall, Lynn Wall, Ernest Wall, Elizabeth Wall, Nathan Wall, Ken Shamrock, Frank Shamrock, Mark Coleman, Randy Couture, Don Frye, Dan Severn, Maurice Smith, Jeff Osborne, John McCarthy, Stephen Quadros, Jack David, Emma, ECW Press in general, "Mr. Showtime" Allan Bassett, Bob Shafto, Dave Meltzer, Joe Silva, Elizabeth Moore, Bruce Buffer, Chee, everyone who has helped me throughout my mixed martial arts writing career, and everyone else who contributed to the book in some form or another.

I'd like to have more people to thank, but I think that's pretty much it.

Introduction

The purpose of this book is to generate discussion and debate about the greatest fighters in UFC history. Nothing more.

The UFC has come a long way in just ten years. Mixed martial arts (MMA) fans and fiends have seen tremendous changes, controversy, happenings, and many amazing athletes since the first UFC event back in November of 1993. UFC, or the Ultimate Fighting Championship, is the most visible mixed martial arts promotion in North America today. It was the first of its kind on this continent, and to this day, it remains the top company promoting the sport in the United States.

This book examines the ten greatest fighters in the history of the UFC. MMA, by its very nature, is a sport that evolves extremely quickly, and after a decade, there have been sufficient developments for us to be able to look back at the fighters who helped to make the UFC what it is today.

So, what makes a fighter great? Or, to be more precise, what makes a fighter the greatest? Nothing. That's the most accurate, most realistic, answer. Determining the greatest fighter in the history of UFC, or of any promotion, time, or place, is virtually impossible. There is no single quality that could instantly and unarguably distinguish a fighter as "the greatest." It's simply not possible.

But it is possible to determine a subjective (that's the key word for this book, by the way) ranking of the greatest fighters based on a series of qualifications. Of course, this prompts the question: upon what qualifications should a ranking of the "greatest" fighters in UFC history be based?

First of all, if you generate a set of qualifications by which to rank these fighters, then you're going to come up with a certain pool of candidates in no particular order. If you were to adjust these qualifications, even slightly, you would, in effect, adjust the list of candidates. This means that, in order to determine the "greatest" fighters, you need to establish a set of qualifications to basically define what "greatest" means. Such a set of qualifications inevitably creates certain boundaries, and the greatest fighter under a certain set of qualifiers is not going to be the greatest fighter under another set of qualifiers. This is one of the fundamental reasons why you can never come up with a definitive ranking of the greatest fighters; the idea itself is flawed at its very roots.

This book, of course, does use a specific set of qualifications to determine which fighters are included, as well as the order in which they are ranked. Before we dive into the qualifications used to determine the top ten fighters in UFC history, it should be noted that any time an exercise as subjective as this is undertaken, it's going to be shaded by opinion. There is no way around that. I will present the set of qualifiers I have come up with, and the top ten fighters ranked according to these qualifiers, but in the end, almost everybody will have a different opinion on whom should be ranked as the greatest fighter in UFC history, even if we're all using the same qualifiers to determine their standing.

In the August 2003 issue of the *Touch of Evil Newsletter*, I went about the task of ranking the thirty greatest fighters in mixed martial arts history based primarily on skill, but also taking box-office power, influence, and accomplishments in MMA (in no particular order) into consideration. I ended up with Mark Coleman as number one on the list. It was a very tough choice to make at the time, and, in my mind, there are easily half a dozen fighters or more who could have been in that top spot.

The flaw with the ranking in *Touch of Evil* was that it was based primarily on skill. This was a genuine weakness because you can't say, for example, that Mark Coleman is far more skilled at wrestling in MMA than Mirko CroCop is at kickboxing in MMA. It's comparing apples and oranges. Because MMA is essentially a melting pot of competitive martial arts, many different styles of fighters compete against each other, and it's unfair (not to mention impossible) to say one particular fighter is better at his style than another fighter whose style may differ but who is in reality just as accomplished in his own domain.

Another flaw in ranking fighters based on skill is the fact that this system is so completely relative. There have been massive advances in MMA in the past decade, so naturally the fighters from the early 1990s were not as skilled as the fighters post-2000, simply because of the sport's natural evolution. Comparing the most skilled fighters of yesteryear to the most skilled fighters of today is like comparing the Royce Gracie of 1994 to the Randy Couture of 2003. Who is superior, Royce in 1994 or Couture in 2003? Who knows? Such a comparison is impossible and unfair to the earlier fighters because modern fighting techniques are so much more advanced.

Yet another flaw in ranking fighters based primarily on skill is the fact that weight determines so much in an MMA bout. Would Tim Sylvia defeat Takanori Gomi if they fought? Probably yes, but does that mean Sylvia is more skilled than Gomi, or does that mean it's just an unfair fight because of the weight and size difference? Determining the most skilled fighter throughout the different weight classes is much like comparing today's fighters to the fighters of MMA's early days. Is Matt Hughes a better fighter at welterweight than Antonio Rodrigo Nogueira is at Heavyweight? Again, who knows?

And even yet another flaw is that, to determine the greatest fighter of all time based on skill, you have to look at whom a particular fighter has fought and defeated. But much of the time, wins and losses are determined by the rules of the fight. Rules are instrumental in determining the outcome of a fight in MMA, and this is something most people simply don't realize. For example, if Royce Gracie fought Mike Tyson in a bout where the rules stated that you could take your opponent down, but you were not allowed to do any groundwork, then Tyson would have a huge advantage because Royce's greatest strength as a fighter would be taken away. If Tyson won that fight, would it make him the better fighter? No, it certainly wouldn't—it would just make him the better fighter under a set of rules that happens to both favor his strengths and undermine those of his opponent. That's an extreme example, but there are many far more subtle examples throughout the history of UFC and MMA, evident in the amount of rule changes that the sport has undergone in different promotions and countries since its inception.

Early on in the development of this book, it was decided that, since this is a ranking of the greatest fighters in the history of the UFC alone, the main qualifier for inclusion must be a fighter's overall importance to the history of UFC and to MMA. For the purposes of this book, "overall importance" consists of a combination of factors: a fighter's positive influence on the development of both UFC and the sport of mixed martial arts in general; a particular athlete's importance to the UFC itself when he was both in and out of his prime as a fighter; his wins, losses, and abilities shown in his UFC fights; and his box-office drawing power and overall contribution to the UFC's bottom line.

Let's take a look at these specific qualifying subcategories and break them down in order of importance.

1. INFLUENCE

This category is given the most weight, since it basically questions whether, if this fighter had never existed, MMA and the UFC itself would be different. Did a particular fighter do something so important to the development of the UFC as a promotion and of MMA as a sport that things might have been completely different today if he had never stepped into the ring? That's the ultimate influence, but influence can mean any number of things. Did a competitor bring a certain style of fighting into the UFC that influenced other fighters to do the same? Did a fighter come up with a new and improved way to train? Did a fighter come along and raise the bar a little higher for everyone who would follow after him by having great fights and displaying a tremendous amount of skill? These are only a few of the things that can be considered influential acts by a fighter; there are certainly many more beyond what are listed here.

2. IMPORTANCE AS A FIGHTER

This category is given a lot of weight, although not as much as the category that defines influence. Importance as a fighter is more specific to UFC (although it can be applied to MMA as a whole), and it refers to how important a particular fighter was to the UFC, both in and out of his prime as a fighter. It's like looking at the "MVPs" in UFC history. How valuable was a certain fighter to the promotion? Value to the promotion can be defined by a fighter's effectiveness as a box-office draw, his performance in headline bouts, and the UFC's success when they built their promotion around this particular fighter. If UFC never built their promotion around a given fighter, that factor was taken into consideration as well. Of course, fighters who were integral parts of UFC during its more profitable years are given weight over fighters who were central to the promotion during its downtime. The better UFC did when built around a particular fighter, the better the fighter fares in this ranking.

3. WINS, LOSSES, RECORD, AND DISPLAYED ABILITY

This qualification certainly deserves to be weighed in this ranking, as it basically measures how good a fighter is at doing what he does. A fighter's record doesn't mean that much because it can be misleading: it's individual wins and losses; who was defeated; and how that counts. For example, Joe Blow may have had an undefeated record of 11–0 in MMA competition, but then he steps into the UFC and fights a top-tier guy at his weight and gets defeated very quickly and very easily. Joe Blow is now 14–1. His record still looks great, and his winning percentage is still great, but since he had no clue when it came to fighting a truly skilled fighter, should he be considered one of the best fighters out there? And let's say that UFC gives Joe Blow another shot against a different, highly skilled challenger, figuring that his first loss might have been a fluke, and Joe Blow gets destroyed again. At 14–2, his record is still great, but he's been defeated twice by top-tier fighters, proving that he doesn't belong at the top level, so what does record mean? Nothing. Wins and losses against top-tier talent both in and outside of UFC are considered in this category, and how well a fighter performs against someone of equal or greater skill is in the end what determines how skilled that fighter is. It's also telling of how complete a fighter is in MMA, because a kickboxer may be great at K-1, but if he has no takedown defense and no understanding of ground-fighting, then he'll be easily defeated in UFC. That doesn't mean he's a bad kickboxer. It just means he's not a complete fighter, and no matter how great he is at kickboxing, to fight against top-tier talent in UFC you have to be a complete fighter.

4. BOX-OFFICE DRAWING POWER

This is the easiest qualifier to measure because it's based on stats and figures, but there's a very long and complicated explanation for how these stats and figures work, so if you're not familiar with how the business of pay-per-view operates, be prepared, because it's not simple, and I'm about to explain it.

Drawing power is basically summed up as meaning whether or not a lot of people will pay money to see a specific person fight. The more people who will pay to see the fighter, the more drawing power that fighter has. That's pretty much the gist of it. Since, as a company, UFC is based on pay-per-view, fighters' drawing power is measured by how well their pay-per-view events do when they are in the headline bout. Pay-per-view success is basically measured by two factors: the number of homes that buy a show, and the buyrate the show gets.

As of this writing, 53.5 million homes in the United States and Canada are equipped with pay-per-view. That number fluctuates regularly and will probably be slightly different by the time you read this. The buyrate of a pay-per-view is the percentage of homes in which a given show is available that actually purchased it. For example, if a UFC pay-per-view was available in 53.5 million homes in the U.S. and 150,000 homes purchased the show, it would be a very high buyrate for the post-SEG UFC. Now, buyrates are reflected in hundredths, which means that a show purchased by 0.01% of the homes in which it is available is referred to as a 1.0 buyrate (0.01 multiplied by 100 equals 1.0). So a show that did 0.0028% of the total homes would be a 0.28 buyrate.

The big difference between the actual number of homes to buy a pay-per-view and the buyrate of the pay-per-view is that the buyrate only reflects a percentage of the total homes the show was available in, meaning that it is not an accurate reflection of the number of people watching a particular pay-per-view, but it is an accurate reflection of the popularity of one particular show or headline bout over another. Look at it this way: in the late 1990s, the UFC was not on a lot of cable systems due to the cable ban caused by political pressure, and therefore, in that era the total number of homes that UFC pay-per-views were available in was very low. In late 1993, UFC started out available in roughly 28 million homes in the U.S. (again, now it's 53.5 million homes because the pay-per-view universe has grown by leaps and bounds over the past ten years). The cable ban continued through the late '90s, so although the overall pay-per-view universe had expanded, UFC was only available in about 12 million homes. Let's say a pay-per-view from the early era of UFC, when shows were available in 28 million homes across the U.S., did a 0.5 buyrate. That would be equal to roughly 140,000 homes buying the show. Now, let's say UFC did a 1.0 buyrate for a show when it was available only in 12 million homes. That's a total of 120,000 homes buying the show. So the first show only did a 0.5 buyrate but was seen in 140,000 homes, compared to the second show, which did a 1.0 buyrate—double the buyrate of the first show—but was seen in 20,000 fewer homes because the second show was less widely available for purchase.

These figures, plus other pay-per-view figures used throughout this book, represent only the United States and Canada, and don't reflect the stats of pay-per-view airings in other countries. Pay-per-view stats and figures are considered, at best, rough estimates. For example, when it is said that UFC 40 was purchased by 150,000 homes, it's just an approximation, not an exact number. Any profits made by UFC would be made basically through pay-per-view and ticket sales. Ticket sales aren't going to be referred to much in this book, because the number of tickets sold for a specific UFC event owes more to the brand name than to any particular fighter on the show, since ticket sales are basically the same whenever UFC returns to a venue they've run before, as long as the promotion's popularity remains more or less at the same level. We know that UFC pay-per-view success is more strongly determined by who is in the headline fight(s), because if people bought UFC shows for UFC's brand name alone, then pay-per-view buyrates would be very similar, instead of fluctuating up and down as they do based on the "big names" in the show. In short, to determine a fighter's drawing power for this book, we will look at the pay-per-view figures discussed above.

FIGHTERS LEFT OUT OF THE BOOK

Determining which fighters made this book's list and which didn't was an excruciating process. As discussed in the Introduction, it's realistically impossible to rank the top ten fighters, and therefore the purpose of the ranking is simply to generate discussion.

Here we'll take a brief look at fighters who were close to making the top ten (some very close), as well as a few others who weren't, and explore the reasons why these fighters didn't make the cut.

Before we discuss these fighters, it should be noted that just being considered for a list like this is an amazing accomplishment in any sport, whether it be football, baseball, hockey, mixed martial arts, or whatever. Many of the fighters listed in this section could easily have been in the top ten, whereas others were unlikely to be considered for the list. But that's not to say that these fighters are "bad," or not as good as those in the top ten. Mixed martial arts is a sport in which, realistically, the best fighter is whoever has the best fight on a given night. For that very reason, there are no absolutes in this book. And even some fighters who aren't listed here, like Murilo Bustamante or BJ Penn, are excellent fighters and athletes whose roles in MMA history should not be discounted. But this is a book of the top ten fighters in UFC history, so it's inevitable that some good fighters didn't make the list.

The fighters are listed alphabetically by last name.

Vitor Belfort. An extremely talented striker and a black belt in Brazilian Jiu Jitsu, Belfort fought in some of the more memorable UFC matches in history, but his heart is questionable, and throughout most of his career he has been considered an underachiever and a "what if" case. His influential impact on UFC and MMA is negligible.

Matt Hughes. Possibly the most dominating champion in UFC history, Hughes had a long run as the UFC Welterweight champion, making five successful title defenses against highly skilled opponents within two years' time. Hughes is also considered one of the top pound-for-pound fighters worldwide in the modern era. The problem with Hughes is that this book looks primarily at influence, and beyond setting the bar a little bit higher as a great fighter and champion, he really hasn't had any influence on the UFC or MMA, and any influence he might have on the sport won't be felt until later. If there were a list of the top ten pound-for-pound fighters in UFC in terms of skill, Hughes would definitely be on it. In a list based on influence, however, Hughes isn't a consideration.

Chuck Liddell. Consistently in the running for the UFC Light-Heavyweight title (the most popular title in the promotion), Liddell is one of the more recognizable faces of the Zuffa-owned UFC. However, he has never held the title, nor has he had a consistent streak of wins over top-tier fighters in his weight division. Ultimately, despite being a great fighter, Liddell has had little, if any, influence on UFC and MMA.

Pat Miletich. This fighter was a very serious contender for the top-ten list. If this book ranked the top eleven fighters in UFC history, Miletich could be number eleven. Realistically, he could just as easily be in the top ten as many of the fighters who actually are. Miletich was a pioneer fighter of the early Lightweight division in UFC; he played a major part in pioneering the independent MMA scene in the United States, a scene that has played a monumental role in the discovery and development of new fighters, and he runs one of the top training camps on the planet today: Miletich Martial Arts. He's also a former UFC Lightweight champion who had a lengthy title run. The main reason why Miletich was left out of the book was that his run as the UFC Lightweight/Welterweight champion saw him defend the title mostly against second-tier opponents, whom he defeated in dull fights. Plus, Miletich lost numerous times on the independent scene, fighting outside of the UFC and not defending his title when he was champion, so his record as champion certainly isn't flawless. Miletich's title run also occurred during the UFC's most unpopular years as a promotion. As a trainer, Miletich might be considered more influential than he ever was as a fighter. His influence on the UFC and on MMA can't be denied, but there are only so many spots available on the list.

Kevin Randleman. A former UFC Heavyweight champion, Randleman is one of the most gifted athletes to ever set foot in any MMA promotion. There are two problems with Randleman, though, and they're big ones. First off, his UFC title run came during a period when UFC was suffering its worst downturn in business and popularity, one reason why he is one of the most unmemorable champions in UFC history. The second major problem with Randleman is that, although he is an incredibly gifted athlete, he hasn't nearly lived up to his potential in this sport, so he's universally considered an underachiever and a disappointment as a fighter.

Marco Ruas. Among the top Brazilian fighters of all time, Ruas is a legend in that country, not to mention one of the top trainers in MMA today. Ruas was a highly skilled fighter on the brutal Brazilian vale tudo scene in the 1980s and early '90s, but by the time he entered the UFC, in 1995, he was thirty-four years old. Although he won the UFC tournament in which he made his debut, he didn't follow it up with anything meaningful, and his career in modern MMA was short because age caught up with him quickly. He is, however, one of the more influential fighters and trainers in all of MMA, but his influence owes to what he did in Brazil, not what he did in UFC.

Bas Rutten. One of the greatest mixed martial artists in the history of the sport, Rutten spent most of his career in Pancrase. He started out with a mixed record, fighting essentially as a pure kickboxer, but he improved in the ground game and eventually went for over four years and twenty-one straight fights without a loss before he retired as an active fighter. Bas is also one of the greatest kickboxers to set foot in MMA, not to mention one of the most charismatic fighters ever. The reason he isn't included here is that he only did two fights in UFC at the tail end of his career, and although he did hold the UFC Heavyweight title, he defeated Kevin Randleman in an extremely close fight and never defended the belt. Bas is one of the greatest, but in a list exclusive to UFC, two fights just aren't enough to get him into the top ten in the promotion's history.

Oleg Taktarov. A very good fighter during the original era of the UFC, Taktarov was in some important matches in that period, including a pay-per-view main event against Ken Shamrock (which went to a very dull time-limit draw). He also won the UFC 6 tournament, defeating the debuting Tank Abbott in the finals in one of the best matches of that era. Taktarov also was a featured fighter on some other early MMA pay-per-view events outside of UFC. Beyond that, he hasn't done much. His style of fighting hasn't changed martial arts over time, and his accomplishments aren't really all that extraordinary, especially considering the higher number of tournaments UFC held at its events in the first few years. As MMA started to evolve, Taktarov was left behind, and he hasn't fought in years, opting instead to pursue a career in acting. Taktarov is best remembered as a decent fighter during the UFC's early days, and that is all.

MIKE LANO

STEPHEN QUADROS

David "Tank" Abbott

There are some fighters whom people just love to hate. Tank Abbott is one of them.

Imagine every stereotype about the drunken bar brawler, a grizzly bear of a man who puts up with nothing from anyone but dishes out as much as he can. Imagine him as a charismatic, bad man, the very definition of an MMA trash-talker, so cocky about his own bar-brawling abilities that MMA fans just want to see the bad man get a taste of his own bad medicine. Other MMA fans just want to see him dish out that medicine, and live vicariously through their drunken hero.

"There's no gray or white. It's black or white. You either hate me or you like me," said Abbott in an interview with *Boxing Insider*. "There's no in-between. That's because I'm honest and that's who I am. I'll tell you the way it is—or the way I think it is. If you don't like it, what are you going to do? If you don't like me, guess what? I probably don't even know who you are."

David Abbott was born on April 26, 1965, in California. He was nicknamed after Tank Murdoch, a character in the Clint Eastwood film *Every Which Way but Loose*, in which Clint plays an underground, professional bare-knuckle fighter, and Murdoch is a legendary bare-knuckle fighter mentioned throughout the film. In sharp contrast to what many people believe about Tank, despite the fact that his image projects the idea of this barbarian ogre, Abbott is actually a very intelligent man with a degree in history from the University of California Long Beach. A very intelligent man who just happens to love booze and brawling.

But, again to the surprise of many, Abbott isn't just a brawler. He started to compete in amateur wrestling when he was nine years old, and continued to wrestle all the way to the collegiate level. That said, Tank's fighting technique in MMA is better described as that of a backstreet brawler than that of an accomplished amateur wrestler. Abbott has also dabbled in amateur boxing. "I trained in a Mexican boxing gym for over twelve years," says Tank in a *WrestleZone Radio* interview. "In fact, I still go down there. All the trainers down there show you how to sit down on your punches and throw some heavy punches because, well, Mexican guys aren't exactly big guys, so they really have to get their body into their punches. There's not too many Mexican heavyweights out there, but they're the ones who pretty much showed me how to throw my punches."

Although the degree to which Tank's street fighting could be a myth perpetuated by Tank himself is up to the discerning fan, the truth is that when Tank first heard of the UFC, he was sitting in a jail cell serving a seven-month sentence. UFC, with its early "no rules" marketing, supposedly banned in most every state, sounded like a perfect match for Tank. At the time, UFC seemed as much out of the Eastwood movie *Every Which Way but Loose* as Tank was.

Through a friend of his, Dave Thomas, Abbott was able to contact Art Davie, one of the founders of UFC and a company bigwig at the time. Davie liked what Thomas had to say about Tank Abbott and his colorful persona and demeanor, and Tank was invited to attend UFC 5 in Charlotte, North Carolina, on April 7, 1995. Staying true to character, Abbott got so drunk on vodka while attending UFC 5 that he lost his ticket for the event and had to be seated elsewhere at the arena.

At the time, the prevailing belief within SEG was that, due to the political pressure UFC was under for being a "dangerous" event, someone like Tank Abbott might not be the best addition to the promotion's competitive roster.

Many inside the company felt that—unlike many of the highly skilled and highly disciplined martial artists who had already competed in UFC—Tank could really hurt someone. Of course, many years and many fights later, that would be proven vastly untrue, since a highly skilled mixed martial artist will defeat a tough, mean street fighter almost every time out. Tank Abbott was largely responsible for debunking the longtime myth of the badass bar brawler who can withstand any sort of punishment and dish out even more, and this is one of his biggest contributions to mixed martial arts, and the main reason why he is placed so highly on a list like this, although that almost certainly was not his goal.

SEG decided to take a risk on Tank, though, and he was booked for the first round of the UFC 6 tournament, held on July 14, 1995. Abbott's first-round opponent was the equally menacing John Matua, a 350-pound Hawaiian smasher.

Although Matua had nearly a hundred-pound weight advantage over Tank, he was the one to get smashed, as Abbott knocked him out in vicious fashion just twenty seconds into the fight. It was quite a sight to see the behemoth Matua so easily knocked out cold. It was also quite a sight to see Tank Abbott rudely mock his downed opponent as he left the octagon. With his vicious knockout power and equally vicious persona, in Tank Abbott a new villain was born.

Since Abbott was basically just a street brawler, and every competitor in the UFC during that era was supposed to represent a technique or style (i.e., Royce Gracie with jiu jitsu, Dan Severn with wrestling, etc.), Abbott was billed as being a "pit fighter," which was a style of fighting made up by SEG in trying to market Abbott with a cool background.

This fight started a trend for Tank Abbott: he was one of the earliest fighters in mixed martial arts who, when he stepped into the octagon, stood a very real chance of knocking his opponent out cold. Although the sport eventually advanced past Tank's skill level, and more dangerous kickboxers such as

Pedro Rizzo and later Mirko "CroCop" Filipovic, surpassed his striking power, Tank was nevertheless one of the very first knockout fighters of MMA. "I have a bar brawling reputation, but I would rather say it's a bar brawling mentality," Abbott tells *WrestleZone Radio*. "I'll fight anybody, I don't care about anything. I've paid my dues on the wrestling mat, in the boxing ring, and in submissions, so I'm not really worried about what people got to bring. They should be worried about what I've got to bring."

Tank's fight against John Matua was also monumental in that it was the first time a UFC competitor wore gloves similar to the eight-ounce gloves used regularly in mixed martial arts today, and Tank was the fighter wearing those gloves. Although gloves would eventually become standard in MMA because of the rule modifications the sport would undergo in later years, Tank was the first fighter to wear such gloves in the octagon.

Abbott had toppled a giant in the first round, and did so again in the second round of the UFC 6 tournament when he stopped the 6'8", 300-pound Paul "The Polar Bear" Varelans in less than two minutes. He pounded Varelans against the fence, with a grin on his face like a kid in a candy store all the while. Although the self-described "anti–martial artist" was only fighting on beer-fueled mayhem and pure bar-brawling abilities, Abbott had made it to the finals of the UFC 6 tournament.

Abbott's opponent for the finals was the skilled Russian fighter Oleg Taktarov, who had defeated Dave Beneteau in less than one minute's time in the first round, then defeated Anthony Macias in just nine seconds in a controversial second-round match widely reported by both corners as fixed. Whether or not Taktarov's second-round victory over Macias was worked, Taktarov had spent a total of sixty-six seconds in the octagon that night. With the high-altitude location of the event in Casper, Wyoming, combined with the fact that, if you just compared the athletic Taktarov to Tank Abbott and his beer belly, odds were that Tank didn't have enough gas in his tank to put up a fight in the tournament finals.

Tank did have enough gas to take the fight to over seventeen minutes in length, delivering Taktarov the fight that he himself claims was the hardest of his life. The altitude did take Tank down a notch, as he started to wear out just a few minutes into the fight, but so did Taktarov, and they battled until the Russian secured a choke, icing Abbott off and winning the tournament. The fight against Taktarov would be considered one of the best and most exciting bouts from that era of mixed martial arts.

Abbott's loss to Taktarov in the UFC 6 tournament finals set another trend for Tank: when it came down to the big fight where the indescribable, known as "heart," had to deliver more than skill, conditioning, or any kind of training or trash-talking a competitor could participate in, Tank would choke, and was ultimately unable to win "the big one" in any UFC tournament.

Abbott returned for his second UFC appearance on December 16, 1995, at the first-ever Ultimate Ultimate tournament in Denver, Colorado. The event featured some of the biggest names and best fighters in UFC at that time, and was based around the idea that everyone in the tournament had been a finalist in a past tournament. Abbott got in because he was, of course, the runner-up against Taktarov in the UFC 6 tournament.

Abbott's first-round opponent for the Ultimate Ultimate was Steve Jennum, a police officer by day, and the UFC 3 tournament champion by night. He had come into the UFC 3 tournament finals as an alternate and won the entire tournament with just one fight, over Harold Howard. The gimmick with this fight was obvious: the ninja cop, Steve Jennum, up against the badass jailbird, Tank Abbott.

Unfortunately for Jennum, Abbott fought the law, and this time, the law didn't win. Tank put a beating on Jennum, submitting him with a simple neck crank in only 1:14 to advance to the second round of the tournament. There he would meet former prized amateur wrestler Dan "The Beast" Severn.

Severn, one of the best fighters of that era in UFC, had been a top collegiate wrestler many moons before. He had learned how to use his weight and wrestling skills to his advantage in MMA competition. Tank, a self-promoted bar brawler, also has a background in amateur wrestling that he doesn't speak of often, and although Severn may have been the more celebrated wrestler of the pair, this fight presented an interesting opportunity to test whether Tank could use his wrestling knowledge to thwart Severn's offense.

Severn punished Tank on the ground for most of the bout, not wanting to fight a standup game against the man with heavy hands. The fight actually went the distance as, for the first time in UFC history, ringside judges had been added to render a decision in case the bout went to the time limit. At UFC 6, Tank had been the first fighter in the UFC to wear kenpo-style gloves, and coincidentally, at the 1995 Ultimate Ultimate, he was in the first-ever UFC fight to go to a decision. Unfortunately for him, Tank ended up on the losing end of a unanimous decision that sent Severn into the finals to defeat Oleg Taktarov and win the tournament.

This was the last time Tank appeared in the octagon for many months as, while attending UFC 8 in Puerto Rico to watch his friend Paul Herrera take on Gary Goodridge (Goodridge knocked Herrera out), Tank got into an altercation with tough jiu jitsu master Allan Goes, with whom Tank had briefly trained prior to his UFC debut. "I waited until between fights, so [Goes] walked back to his section," recalls Tank. "When he saw me walk over towards him, he started fucking backing off. I was like, 'Where are you going now, you little fucking bitch, what are you doing?' So it turned into a big melee."

At the time, the UFC was under intense political pressure and scrutiny from powerful people who would have liked to see it disappear. During Tank's altercation with Goes at UFC 8, Elaine McCarthy, the wife of UFC ref John McCarthy, berated Tank's girlfriend for cheering him on. Tank, not one to mince words, told Elaine McCarthy what he thought of her in a not-so-nice way, and subsequently John threatened to leave the promotion unless Tank was fired. To calm things down, Art Davie put Abbott on a paid suspension, and SEG programmer David Isaacs wrote an apology letter to the McCarthys that Tank signed. Due to the incident, Tank didn't fight in UFC again until UFC 11 in September of 1996, nearly a year after his last fights at the Ultimate Ultimate in December 1995.

The most interesting outcome of this silly altercation was that Tank's return to the octagon for the UFC 11 pay-per-view was built around the idea of his return to the UFC for the first time in nearly a year in the opposite tournament bracket for the show of the UFC 10 tournament champion, Mark Coleman. Since Coleman had just made his debut at UFC 10, Tank was arguably the biggest name and box-office drawing card at the event.

After making quick work of Sam Adkins in the first round of the tournament by submitting him with a neck crank, Tank came up against the fat man, Scott Ferrozzo, a training partner of Don Frye's who was very eager to fight Tank.

Ferrozzo wasn't an especially good fighter, even for that era of the UFC. He weighed more than 300 pounds, and in his debut at UFC 8, he had lost to Jerry Bohlander, a man nearly half his size. After having defeated Sam Fulton in an alternates fight for the UFC 11 tournament, Ferrozzo's fight against Tank was only the third UFC fight of his career.

Tank should have been able to defeat Ferrozzo. There was no reason for him to lose this fight. But he did. Abbott had assumed that he would fight Bohlander in the second round of this tournament, but an injured Bohlander pulled out of the tournament after winning a long decision against Fabio Gurgel in the first round. Since Ferrozzo had won his alternates fight, he came in to replace Bohlander.

Abbott and Ferrozzo were both basically brawlers, so fans expected a war of big men and heavy leather, but Tank had gone into the tournament with a bad knee, and had to work around that. Abbott versus Ferrozzo ended up being a long and fairly slow fight, as both guys battled up against the fence for most of the regulation period and for a chunk of the overtime. Abbott found himself on the losing end of a decision. Ferrozzo was actually too exhausted to continue on in the tournament, and Mark Coleman, who had won his first- and second-round fights, won the UFC 11 tournament by default, without actually facing anyone in the finals.

Abbott's loss to Ferrozzo was further proof that, when it comes down to the wire, Tank is a guy to bet against. Losing the fight against Ferrozzo was Tank's first disappointing performance at UFC 11. His second disappointing performance was at the box office.

At the time, SEG loved Tank Abbott, because he was everything that the casual fan wanted out of a fighter: someone who talked trash, drank beer, and had basically stepped off of a barstool and into the octagon. That should have meant money to SEG. But it didn't. Despite popular belief about what draws money at the box office, Tank Abbott was never a box-office drawing card throughout his UFC career, nor did this improve when he ventured into pro wrestling for WCW (although Tank was misused in the latter company).

UFC 11 drew a 0.45 buyrate on pay-per-view, and although that was up from the 0.43 drawn by the previous UFC event, it was disappointing in comparison to earlier UFC events—headlined by superstars Ken Shamrock, Royce Gracie, and Dan Severn—that had drawn close to 1.0. Furthermore, because UFC 11 was built around the idea of Tank, a should-be superstar, returning to the octagon, it should have done a better number. But it didn't, because Tank was not a drawing card.

But Tank did continue to compete in UFC for SEG. He was one of eight fighters selected to compete in the December 1996 Ultimate Ultimate tournament.

One of the most anticipated fights at the 1996 Ultimate Ultimate was between Tank Abbott and Ken Shamrock. Shamrock versus Abbott was not booked for the first round of the tournament, however, as Shamrock was booked against Brian Johnston and Tank against Cal Worsham in the first round. But it was expected that Ken and Tank would defeat their respective first-round opponents to meet in the second round.

Tank had a long-standing feud with Shamrock, dating back to when Tank had made some ignorant remarks about Shamrock trainee Jerry Bohlander when Bohlander pulled out of the UFC 11 tournament. From there, everything just snowballed between the quick-tempered Shamrock and the quick-witted Tank. Their mutual dislike is now legendary.

"He's not a fighter, he's a joke," said Tank when interviewed for Clyde Gentry's book *No Holds Barred: Evolution*. "Let me explain something to you. I'm in the professional wrestling business. You wanna know what the number one fucking claim by professional wrestling is? I want to be famous for something that's easy! Ken Shamrock wants to be famous and that's his whole motivation in life. He was a professional wrestler before he ever got into professional fighting. He's an absolute jokeaholic. He's a steroided, one hundred and eight pound joke! He ain't nothing but a joke. He had two times to fight me and he ran! And you want to know what? A fighter does not care about losing."

But before Abbott and Shamrock could meet, Tank had to get past Worsham in the first round. The knee injury Tank had suffered before UFC 11 had been fixed prior to the 1996 Ultimate Ultimate, enabling him to train harder and lose weight for this show, and he looked to be in decent shape for his body type. Abbott looked decent against Worsham, too, and their fight was memorable in that Tank actually tried to pick Worsham up and toss him out of the octagon. Although the tactic failed, Tank did slam Worsham down the canvas, and eventually finished him in less than three minutes. A post-fight brawl nearly erupted as, after Worsham submitted to the pounding he was taking from Tank and referee John McCarthy broke them apart, Tank threw an extra punch for good measure. Worsham freaked out, but McCarthy kept the peace, and the situation blew over.

Tank moved on into the second round of the 1996 Ultimate Ultimate but, unfortunately for UFC fans across the globe, Ken Shamrock didn't, as he had broken his hand to defeat Brian Johnston in their first-round fight. Because of this, Tank's opponent for the second round was tournament alternate Steve Nelmark. One of the greatest highlight-reel scenes in UFC history occurred when Tank backed Nelmark up against the fence, knocking him out at only 1:03 of the fight with a wicked right hand that literally folded Nelmark to the ground in a heap, his brain shut off by the powerful blow.

So far that night, Abbott had competed in less than four minutes' worth of fighting in two matches, and he was on his way to the finals to take on Don Frye, arguably the best UFC fighter from that era.

Frye versus Abbott was an interesting, albeit brief, altercation. Frye had defeated Gary Goodridge in the first round of the tournament, and he'd also defeated Mark Hall in the second round in a quick and controversial bout that many insiders feel was worked. In fact, not only was this the second time Tank made it to the finals of a UFC tournament, but it was the second time that his opponent in the finals would be accused of doing a worked fight to get to that point.

Early in the fight, Frye made the mistake of deciding to stand and duke it out with Tank. To show what kind of heavy hitter Tank was, Frye had competed as a professional boxer, whereas Tank was just a barroom brawler with some boxing training, but he was able to out-duel Frye on their feet. For a few brief seconds, it looked like Tank might put Frye to sleep, but Don Frye isn't known as one of the toughest men on the planet for nothing; Tank wasn't able to knock him out. Actually, Frye accidentally stepped on Tank's foot, causing Tank to trip, and Frye was then able to tap him out on the ground with a rear naked choke. The fight was all over in eighty-two seconds. Abbott had again come up short in the finals of a UFC tournament. It was the last time Tank would be a UFC tournament finalist.

Tank's next battle in the UFC was against then-rising star Vitor Belfort, a young fighter many remarked had the fastest hands in UFC history up to that point. When he pummeled his opponents down to the canvas, his fists were like pistons, smashing the leather of his gloves against his foe's skull. And not only was Belfort a feared striker, he was also an accomplished grappler—although he rarely showed it. Belfort had won a tournament at UFC 12 and was undefeated in MMA at that point in his career. Heading into their war at UFC 13 on May 10, 1997, many felt that Abbott would be Belfort's toughest test yet.

It turned out to be a pretty speedy war, as Abbott clearly didn't approach Belfort's level of skill, and Belfort's fists ate him alive in only fifty-two seconds. Although Abbott had real knockout power in UFC's early days, a new breed of strikers with a skill level higher than what he could ever attain had entered the sport, and with this fight, it became clear that Tank's era as an upper-tier fighter in the UFC was over.

Tank's career in the UFC wasn't over yet, however. Although he had lost his last two fights against Frye and Belfort, he got a shot at Maurice Smith's UFC Heavyweight title at UFC 15 on October 17, 1997, coming in as a last-minute replacement for Dan Severn. Ironically, Tank had originally been booked to take on Kimo at the debut PRIDE show in Japan just six days before UFC 15, but his criminal record made it hard for him to get into Japan, and PRIDE actually got Severn to replace him. Severn and Kimo ended up going to a long, dull draw. Severn injured himself in the fight, and had to pull out of his UFC fight against Smith just days before the event was to happen. UFC gave Tank—rumored to be on a rare $5,000-a-month salary from SEG (most MMA promotions pay fighters per fight)—the call, and Abbott went into the octagon against Smith tremendously overweight and out of shape.

"Everybody that comments on my cardio, it's because I got called at short notice. 'Will you fill in?' No one would fill in at short notice [for] Maurice Smith, nobody. So they had to call me up," says Tank in a *Boxing Insider* interview. "I said, 'Sure, I'll do it.' I went and did it and showed up. Three days—they called me on Tuesday, and I was fighting on Friday and I wasn't training at all. I was drinking."

Although Tank's cardio conditioning for the fight was terrible, he still fought for over eight minutes until, at 8:08 of the fight, he'd basically had enough and tapped out due to a barrage of leg kicks from Smith. He now had three losses against three very skilled fighters in a row.

Tank didn't take much time off, though, and he actually managed to get into Japan to compete on UFC's first Ultimate Japan show on December 21, 1997. Tank was part of a four-man tournament on the show, which also included his first-round opponent Yoji Anjoh, and in the opposite bracket were Extreme Fighting veteran Marcus "Conan" Silveira (making his UFC debut) and Kazushi Sakuraba (who would later become a larger-than-life legend in Japan).

Tank had a hard time putting Anjoh away in their lengthy fight, but he ended up defeating Anjoh via decision. Tank injured his hand in the bout, so he was unable to advance to the finals. Sakuraba ended up winning the tournament by defeating Silveira when their fight was restarted later in the night, as the ref, John McCarthy, had stopped their original bout prematurely.

On May 15, 1998, at UFC 17, Tank returned and stopped Hugo Duarte in only forty-three seconds. Despite the quick victory, Tank's UFC career was quickly winding down. After a rumored fight against Gary Goodridge at UFC 19 that never actually happened, Tank's last fight in the promotion for many years took place on October 16, 1998, at UFC's Ultimate Brazil in Sao Paulo, where Abbott met another highly skilled striker, Pedro Rizzo, who knocked Tank out cold at 8:07 of the bout.

The UFC was losing steam because of the cable ban that had relegated them to minimal exposure on pay-per-view, so many top UFC stars were jumping ship to PRIDE in Japan, or other popular pro wrestling promotions, like WWF, WCW, New Japan, and others. After his loss to Rizzo in late 1998, Abbott signed a deal to work as a professional wrestler with World Championship Wrestling (WCW).

Abbott's WCW run was largely a flop, mainly due to the fact that WCW, as a promotion, was going downhill very quickly at the time. In the mid-'90s,

WCW made more money than any other wrestling promotion—including Vince McMahon's WWF—had ever made in the history of the industry. But mismanagement and office politics had destroyed their momentum, sending them right to the bottom of the industry and eventually out of business. Abbott, a terrible pro wrestler with zero experience in the field, wasn't booked well by the company, so he never got over with the WCW audience to the degree that he might have. Although, in the midst of a power struggle between Vince Russo, then a head writer in WCW, and others in the company office, Tank was nearly made WCW World Champion, for the most part, his run there was a flop.

When WCW went out of business in March 2001, Tank had been working in WCW's developmental territory (their "farm league") and at the Power Plant training facility. It was actually a blessing for Tank that WCW went under, as he, like much of the other talent employed by the promotion, still had a hefty contract that had to be paid off by AOL-Time Warner, WCW's parent company, before they went under. Tank ended up spending months doing nothing inside the pro wrestling and MMA industries, just waiting for his wrestling contract with AOL-Time Warner to expire. Essentially, he was given a very lengthy, very well-paid vacation.

His vacation ended in November of 2002, at UFC 40—the most-purchased pay-per-view under the current UFC ownership—when, to the surprise of many and the delight of some, it was announced that Tank Abbott would return to compete in UFC after four years away from the sport.

No one really gave Tank much of a chance, because MMA had advanced so much since Abbott's last fight that even talent like Rizzo and Vitor Belfort, who had easily handled him back in the late '90s, didn't compare to the new top heavyweights. Plus, Abbott was much older, couldn't possibly be in as good shape as he had been years earlier, and had been untested for many years.

"The whole premise of that show was so smart, if you think back on it," says Tank in an interview with Sherdog.com on the SEG days of UFC compared to the present. "Little guys fighting big guys. People want to see people get their asses kicked. 'No we want to see martial arts.' They don't want to see this shit! 'Cross-training, scientific, it's the double sweet science.' Dumbass, do you want to make some money? Or do you just want to pretend you're tough and get some idiots jacking you off, going, 'You're the shit. What are you on, what do you do?'"

He was tested, however, against young heavyweight submissions master Frank Mir, at UFC 41 in New Jersey on February 28, 2003. As nearly universally predicted, Mir was able to submit Tank very quickly (just forty-six seconds in), with a toe hold.

The loss was the start of a pathetic streak both for Tank and for Zuffa, UFC's parent company, which had brought Tank back into the fold. Tank continually lost very quickly in UFC, despite the fact that Zuffa had decided to pay him $150,000 per fight, which made him one of the highest-paid fighters in the company. The people at Zuffa had thought Tank would be a major pay-per-view draw, not unlike Ken Shamrock, who had returned to tremendous pay-per-view success. Sadly, though, Tank bombed at the box-office that year, and never headlined a UFC pay-per-view with a buyrate better than mediocre. He also fell short as a live gate draw, although Zuffa saw the huge crowd at UFC 41 as evidence of his drawing power (overlooking the fact that UFC had drawn well in Atlantic City in the past without Tank on the card).

Nevertheless, Tank competed in two more fights for the Zuffa-owned UFC, the first of them against his old rival, Kimo, at UFC 43 in Las Vegas on June 6, 2003. The fight had been nearly a decade in the making, as it was hearing about Kimo fighting Royce Gracie at UFC 3 that originally got Tank interested in competing in the promotion, and they had been booked to fight each other at the debut PRIDE show years earlier in Japan, but that had never happened because of Tank's problems getting into the country at that time.

The idea behind Tank's fight with Kimo (who hadn't competed in UFC since March of 1998) was that it would give Tank's image a makeover, since it was assumed that Kimo would probably have degenerated since 1998, but his name still had value from his past in UFC, and he'd give Tank an easy and impressive win.

Not quite. Kimo easily took Tank down to the ground in less than two minutes to submit him with a choke. After the fight, Kimo gave Tank a kiss on the cheek. Earlier in the year, after Frank Mir had tapped him out at UFC 41, Tank had been able to get some of his heat back by getting on the house microphone and challenging Mir to a brawl down at the bar after the bout. There were no bar-fight challenges or excuses after this loss to Kimo, however. It was an embarrassing display both for Abbott and for Zuffa, as they had paid Tank $150,000 for the 119-second fight.

The last fight on Tank's three-fight deal with Zuffa was against Wes "Cabbage" Correira at UFC 45 on November 21, 2003. A striker with a great chin, Cabbage isn't considered a top heavyweight fighter, but UFC booked him because they were looking for someone to stand and brawl with Abbott. And Cabbage did just that, finishing the fight at 2:14 by opening up a cut on Tank. The match was nearly marred by a post-fight brawl between both corners, and later Tank tried to claim that the doctor who stopped the fight had made him lose, but the fact is Tank was a beaten man.

It was rumored that Tank would fight Ken Shamrock in June 2004, but he didn't sign a new deal with Zuffa, opting instead to take some time off back home in California. This leads mixed martial arts fans to question whether the long-standing feud between Shamrock and Abbott will ever be resolved. "I'll be fighting when I'm seventy if I can," says Tank in a Boxing Insider interview. "If I'm still alive. I'll go down fighting all the other whippersnappers; they can kick my ass. I'll get my digs in, though."

Tank lost seven of his last nine bouts and all three of his fights in a less-than-stellar run under the Zuffa-owned UFC, so from a fighting standpoint, the last few years of his career were disastrous. However, it wasn't the last few years that made Tank such an influential part of mixed martial arts and UFC history. He had already proven that a very tough man with heavy hands simply could not defeat a well-trained martial artist, no matter how tough that man claimed to be. The first villain of the UFC, Tank played an important role in the characterization of mixed martial arts. He helped to define what people really wanted to watch, as the fact that his pay-per-view buyrate draws never quite lived up to expectations showed that MMA fans don't really want to see charismatic brawlers with minimal skill; they want to see charismatic athletes with real skill and personality. This certainly wasn't his goal, but by being the "anti-martial artist," Tank proved what the real martial artist could do.

Maurice Smith

With a fighting career that realistically spans twenty-five years, Maurice Smith will be remembered as one of the top kickboxers to come into MMA during the first wave of fighters in the early '90s. He found success with Pancrase first, then with Extreme Fighting, and after that with UFC.

Smith was born on December 13, 1961, in Seattle, Washington, where he was also raised. After seeing Bruce Lee's martial arts displays in the movie *Chinese Connection* at the age of thirteen, Smith, like so many other fighters of his generation, was inspired to take up martial arts. Smith studied tae kwon do, karate, and wing chun and eventually made his way into the world of kickboxing.

"I started martial arts when I was a kid because I was going to get into a fight with this kid, and I ran away," said Smith in an interview conducted for this book. "I didn't like that feeling. So that is how I got started in martial arts. Now I have closure for that, now I fight! I got over that problem. Then once I started fighting it just kind of went on from there. I didn't plan it that way."

In September of 1980, at age eighteen, Maurice made his kickboxing debut in Seattle. He competed in seven amateur fights, compiled a record of 7–0, and unofficially became the Light-Heavyweight champion of Washington State. There was no one else left for him to fight in the Pacific Northwest as an amateur, so Smith decided to turn pro.

His first pro fight was against then–Canadian WKC (World Kickboxing Council) Light-Heavyweight champion Tony Morelli in Vancouver on March

4, 1982, in a non-title fight. Smith lost the seven-round fight, and although he went the distance to a decision, he was not yet ready for such a fight, although he was developing the tools that would one day put him in the class of legendary kickboxers.

Smith began to gas out in the second round of his bout against Morelli. This proved ironic in retrospect, as nearly two decades later, Smith's influence on the way mixed martial artists conditioned themselves was nothing less than major. His desire had carried him to the decision against Morelli, but he had learned a vital lesson: if he really wanted to make it in this business, then he would have to change his whole attitude about training.

That night, on the two-hour drive home from British Columbia, Smith decided that he wanted to be a fighter, and Morelli would be his stepping-stone to a world championship.

Fourteen months later, in Hawaii, they rematched for the WKC Light-Heavyweight title. Smith knocked Morelli out in the seventh round with a roundhouse to the head, ending the fight and winning the WKC Light-Heavy-weight title.

About three months after the fight in Hawaii, Smith got a call to go to Japan for a non-title fight against legendary WKA kickboxing light-heavy-weight Don "The Dragon" Wilson. Smith took Wilson to the full eleven rounds. Having only fought in five professional kickboxing bouts before he faced Wilson, Smith had started to turn some heads in the kickboxing world.

Later that year, Smith moved up a weight to try for the WKA Heavy-weight championship, then held by Travis Everett of Mexico. Using a strategy of low kicks, Maurice defeated Travis for the WKA World Heavyweight title in Mexico City. Smith now held both WKA Heavyweight and WKC Light-Heavyweight titles.

In 1984, Smith competed in Holland, where he had an epiphany about kickboxing technique. Holland is known as the second home of Muay Thai, which wasn't being practiced in many parts of the world then. Smith fought a Dutch fighter named Marcel Swank, who won the fight via knockout in the first round. Smith noticed something different about the way the Dutch kickboxed, in comparison to the way he and all other Americans did. Everything was different in Holland: the way the fighters threw low kicks, the audience's attitude, and the level of electricity the competitors brought to the fight, whether they were "C" class or "A" class fighters.

In the locker room that night, Smith asked an English fighter named Ronnie Green and his trainer if they could show him something. The two of them spent about an hour with Smith, explaining all the fine details on how to throw and block low kicks. Although Maurice had employed the technique of throwing low kicks prior to this, the European fighters were especially skilled in this technique. They were able to show Smith some new tricks, and he sucked it all up like a sponge. When he went back to his hotel, he was excited like a kid in a candy store. Smith now had one step above the other American fighters: they didn't know anything about throwing a low kick the way he did, nor did they know how to properly block them.

Smith had been fighting for many years by the time the WKA became popular in Japan, and as one of the top fighters in the organization, he was led directly into the world of Japanese pro wrestling. His pro wrestling debut was with the UWF, a shoot-style pro wrestling group then on a huge tear of popularity in Japan. They were looking for a kickboxer with a legitimate reputation to feature on one of their major events.

On November 29, 1989, Smith did a match in the UWF at the Tokyo Dome, knocking out talented up-and-coming wrestler Minoru Suzuki in a shoot-style pro wrestling undercard bout. The show, headlined by pro wrestler Akira Maeda defeating European judo champion Willie Wilhelm in a worked match, was the biggest in the UWF's history up to that point, selling out the Tokyo Dome to 60,000 fans paying $2.9 million. The show set an all-time record gate for pro wrestling worldwide up to that point, as well as the record for highest live attendance to a Japanese pro wrestling event, although both of those records have since been broken. It was also the very first time a pro wrestling event had sold out the Tokyo Dome.

Smith competed in another shoot-style pro wrestling match in Japan, headlining the Tokyo Dome on October 4, 1992, against Masakatsu Funaki, who went on to become one of the founders and major names of Pancrase. Funaki and Smith went to a draw in their bout, which took place in front of 40,800 fans paying $1.5 million.

In 1993, karate master and businessman Kazuyoshi Ishii founded a new major kickboxing promotion in Japan, K-1, combining elements of many standup striking martial arts, including but not limited to kickboxing, karate, tae kwon do, and Muay Thai. Built on the idea of using top-level athletes in legitimate kickboxing matches, the promotion held a pro wrestling philosophy for building up feuds and booking television. Ishii had learned the art of pro wrestling booking from working in the front office of RINGS, a major promotion in Japan at that time. Over the years, K-1 has grown to become a national sport in Japan and a staple for Japanese network television, and the K-1 year-end Grand Prix tournament is now a legendary sporting event in that country, along the lines of the World Series or the Super Bowl in North America.

The first K-1 Grand Prix was held on April 30, 1993, and Maurice Smith was part of it, along with legendary kickboxers Masaaki Satake, Branco Cikatic, Ernesto Hoost, and Peter Aerts, among others.

Smith's first-round opponent was Japanese fighter Toshiyuki Atokawa, who had lost in his K-1 debut earlier that year. Smith defeated Atokawa via unanimous decision, and moved into the tournament semifinals.

There he met the man arguably considered the greatest kickboxer of all time: Ernesto Hoost. This event was also Hoost's K-1 debut. He would go on to make a legend for himself in Japan by winning the K-1 Grand Prix tournament numerous times, becoming a major sports television star in that country.

Hoost had defeated the equally legendary Peter Aerts via a close majority decision in the first round of the tournament. Smith versus Hoost didn't get that far, though, as Hoost knocked Smith out at 1:18 of the third round. This sent Hoost into the finals, where he was knocked out in the first round by tournament winner Branco Cikatic (whom Smith would actually fight years later under MMA rules in PRIDE). These two fights, against Atokawa and Hoost, were Smith's only K-1 competitions until mid-1998, after Smith had made a much bigger name for himself in the UFC.

Smith debuted with Pancrase on their third show, held at the Kobe World Commemoration Hall on November 8, 1993. "At that time, it was a business deal because they wanted to promote their sport," says Smith on how he got started with Pancrase. "They more or less just made me an offer."

Smith stopped Suzuki, one of the biggest native stars in the Japanese promotion, at 0:52 of the third round, making his Pancrase debut a huge success. Suzuki and Smith were rematched on May 31, 1994. In the rematch, both fighters were to wear gloves in the first and third rounds, and only Smith would wear gloves in the fifth. However, Suzuki secured an armbar, and Smith tapped out at 0:36 of the third round, so they never got to the fifth.

The submission loss to Suzuki was a precursor of things to come for the kickboxer in Pancrase, as he would be submitted three more times while fighting for the organization. "At the time I fought in Pancrase, I didn't have any real experience in grappling," admits Smith.

Built on a pro wrestling foundation, Pancrase featured many pro wrestling rules. For example, closed-fisted punches were not allowed to the head, which of course would be detrimental to the fighting style of a kickboxer like Smith. "That was the main thing, it had to be open hand," says Smith. "But since that was the rule then, it wasn't in my best interest to do it at that point. There are certain differences you have in punching with a closed fist and with the palm of your hand."

Although Smith had picked up a lot of knowledge about submissions wrestling technique while doing shoot-style pro wrestling for UWF and PWFG, this kind of technique was primarily for worked matches, and Smith's fights in Pancrase were legit. Furthermore, for the most part, Smith was a pure kickboxer at the time. He lacked knowledge of not only how to use submissions, but also how to defend against them. Because of this, he ended up posting a losing 3–4 record while fighting in Pancrase.

"Pancrase gave me some familiarity with the sport," says Smith. "But [fighting in MMA in North America] just kind of happened, and it wasn't really planned out."

In Pancrase, Smith's kickboxing skills were effective against opponents with lower-quality standup skills, however. Smith was entered into the first round of the King of Pancrase title tournament on December 16, 1994. The entire tournament took place over two back-to-back nights. It was the first time in modern history that a pro wrestling promotion featured a world champion who had won his title and defended it in legitimate matches, and Smith would have a chance to become that champion.

In the first round of the tournament, Smith was able to knock out Takaku Fuke at 2:48 to advance into the second round, where he met Pancrase's top foreign star: Ken Shamrock.

Shamrock ended up submitting Maurice at 4:23 of the fight, and this sent Shamrock into the second night of action. Smith lost his chance at the King of Pancrase championship, but he later became friends with Ken, and the two swapped training tips until Shamrock left the MMA world for a number of years by signing with the WWF in early 1997. This connection eventually led Smith to train with Frank Shamrock, who would have a tremendous influence on his career a few years down the road.

Smith's next fight in Pancrase, on May 13, 1995, was also a loss via submission, this time to another kickboxer, Bas Rutten, who was becoming a submissions master. Rutten was able to knee-bar Smith for the tap out just 2:10 into the fight. It was the first of two fights between Smith and Rutten in Pancrase, and the first of two losses for Smith. "When I fought Bas, I really wasn't into the submission part," Smith explains in an interview for Sherdog.com. "I was more or less going in there to help promote Pancrase. I didn't really have much submission skills at the time, and I was just beginning to understand them. I was starting to learn it, so when I fought Bas, he beat me because he had some skills that I didn't."

Smith came back with a win, though, at the 1995 Pancrase Anniversary Show, held at Sumo Hall, this time via knockout over King of Pancrase tournament finalist Manabu Yamada at 1:46 into the second round of their fight. Not only was Yamada knocked out at the end of the fight, but he also suffered a broken arm during the fight.

His knockout victory over Yamada led Smith to another fight against Bas Rutten. This time, though, it was for the King of Pancrase title, which Rutten had won from Minoru Suzuki in the main event of the 1995 Pancrase Anniversary Show. This fight didn't last much longer than their first, as Rutten was able to submit Smith with a choke at just 4:34 into the bout. Smith lost his chance at the King of Pancrase title in his final fight in Pancrase.

At this point, Smith had decided to make his ultimate fighting (a more accurate label for MMA back then) debut in North America, but just not with the UFC. Although UFC had contacted Smith to come in and compete while he was helping Ken Shamrock to prepare for his fight against Dan Severn at UFC 6, Smith had turned the offer down, feeling that he was not complete enough as a fighter to compete in the UFC at that moment.

But on October 18, 1996, Smith was ready, and he made his North American debut at Extreme Fighting 3. Extreme Fighting had decided to put together a four-man tournament for their newly created Heavyweight title; the first-round fights would take place at Extreme Fighting 3, and the finals would take place at the next event.

Smith's opponent in the first round was the massive Brazilian Jiu Jitsu specialist Marcus "Conan" Silveira. To prepare, Smith trained heavily in ground fighting with Frank Shamrock, and they drilled over and over how to defend against a jiu jitsu fighter's submissions. Although he was still seen primarily as a kickboxer, by the time this fight was over, Smith would have proven himself to be more complete as a fighter.

Smith's training with Frank Shamrock, and later with both Shamrock and Tsuyoshi Kohsaka as "The Alliance," was pivotal in his career, and formed a major piece of MMA history. Frank Shamrock is largely credited as the fighter who brought cardio conditioning, along with strategy and cross-training, to the forefront of mixed martial arts, and forever changed the sport.

During the fight, Silveira took Smith down right out of the gate, and Smith went into the guard, but near the end of the first round, Smith surprised everyone by reversing the jiu jitsu master and ending up on top of him. Smith was able to use his newfound grappling skills to frustrate Silveira, and as the fight wore on, Silveira grew increasingly exhausted as he tried to get something going against Smith.

In the third round, Smith started to tag Silveira with hard leg kicks, until Silveira dropped his hands low to block the kicks, and Smith nailed him with a highlight reel–style knockout kick to the side of the head, finishing both Conan and the fight. It was a landmark fight in MMA, because a kickboxer had knocked out a black belt in jiu jitsu, and had been able to do so because he had trained both specifically for the fight and in grappling techniques in general.

The next Extreme Fighting show, on March 28, 1997, was the last show Extreme Fighting would ever hold, as the cable ban on MMA shows would soon kill nearly every MMA promotion in North America. The four-man heavyweight tournament finals were scheduled for this show, and would feature Mo Smith against Kazunari Murakami.

Murakami, a popular wrestler in New Japan Pro Wrestling (who still competed in MMA in Japan from time to time), had defeated another pro wrestler, Bart Vale, in the first round of the tournament back at Extreme Fighting 3. Smith now had a chance to win his first major title in MMA.

Murakami knocked Smith down at the start of the fight with a palm strike, but Smith was able to get back to his feet by reversing Murakami and getting out of his guard. Smith got even with Murakami, using a barrage of kicks to his leg while Murakami just lay against the fence. This went on for under a minute, until Smith stepped back, let Kazunari stand up, and brought the fight back to its feet.

Then it happened. Many consider it one of the greatest knockouts in MMA history up to that point in time. Smith delivered an overhand right, and Murakami went down. The fight was over.

Smith had done what many at that time thought wasn't possible: he was the first kickboxer to come into MMA and win a major North American title in the sport. It was a landmark showcase of fighting in MMA, as prior to this, the sport had been dominated by grapplers, not strikers. Although it was realistically Smith's training in grappling with Frank Shamrock that had taken him so far in Extreme Fighting, he was the first guy with a kickboxing background to reach this level of success in MMA in North America.

With the cable ban in place in early 1997, however, Extreme Fighting became an unprofitable pay-per-view franchise and closed down after this show. Smith never had a chance to defend the Extreme Fighting Heavyweight title that he had won by defeating Silveira and then Murakami. Smith did, however, get a chance to fight for an even bigger title in an even more important fight when he fought, and defeated, Mark Coleman in UFC.

Smith's win over Mark Coleman at UFC 14 was ultimately the fight that made Smith's career. Coleman had been dominating the UFC ever since his debut at UFC 10. He'd won that event's tournament by destroying Don Frye in the finals. Coleman went on to win the UFC 11 tournament, and then had quickly defeated Dan Severn at UFC 12 to win the UFC Heavyweight title. Undefeated at the time, Coleman seemed unstoppable.

A top-tier amateur wrestler, Coleman had placed seventh in the 100-kilogram freestyle wrestling category at the 1992 Olympic Games in Barcelona. He was also a three-time freestyle wrestling gold medalist in the Pan Am Championship, and an NCAA Division I champion at 190 pounds in 1988. In MMA, a great wrestler will almost always defeat a great kickboxer because the kickboxer has no tools once the wrestler gets him off his feet, as the wrestler almost always will do. To say the odds against Maurice Smith defeating Mark Coleman were long would be an understatement. "I was basically a 'striker' fighter playing his game," says Smith.

There was no love lost between Smith and Coleman. Smith had made a comment in a pre-fight interview about Coleman punching like a girl, and this didn't sit well with Coleman. Coleman also outweighed Smith by twenty-five pounds or so, and the general strategy for the fight was that, when Coleman took Smith down, Coleman would use his power to keep Smith down, so Smith wouldn't get a chance to knock Coleman out on their feet—his best chance to win the bout.

The factor that made the difference in this fight was conditioning. If a fighter doesn't have proper conditioning for a fight, then no matter how powerful or superior he may be, he will almost invariably lose if the other fighter can go the distance. You can't fight when you're exhausted.

All of his easy wins over top talent had left Coleman overconfident and complacent. Instead of taking Mo Smith seriously, training hard, and conditioning himself for the fight, Coleman spent his time partying. He didn't train at all. He had no game plan.

Smith trained. And he had a game plan. He worked with Frank Shamrock again for the fight, training hard to improve his grappling skills to combat the choke that Coleman had used to finish off many of his prior opponents. Smith conditioned for the fight. Coleman did not. That was the difference.

The bout took place on July 27, 1997. Immediately into the fight, as most expected, Coleman took Smith down to the ground. It looked like the fight would go according to predictions. Coleman was also eventually able to get side-mount, and later, full mount. Although he had opportunities for submissions on the ground, Coleman was a novice with submissions and wasn't able to secure any.

Coleman gassed quickly. Smith got back to his feet, changing the pace of the fight. Coleman kept resting his hands on his knees, clearly exhausted, with nothing left in the tank. He got a chance to rest when the ref stopped the fight briefly to warn Smith about a foul he had nearly committed: Coleman had shot for another takedown, but was slow in doing it, and Smith nearly kicked him in the head. In UFC, it's illegal to kick someone in the head when he is on the ground, and it was unclear whether or not Coleman was standing or on the ground at that moment.

The rest didn't help Coleman much, as he was still gassed. Smith tagged him with a few leg kicks, but Coleman, a world-class wrestler, still managed to take Smith down and ended up in his guard. Coleman was so tired, though, that Smith eventually reversed him to bring the fight back to a standing game.

The regulation period for the fight ended as per the UFC's time limits of the era, and both fighters were given a rest before each of the three-minute-long overtimes. By the second overtime, Smith was handling Coleman on their feet, and, showing just how gassed Coleman was, at one point when Smith went for a kick, he slipped, but Coleman was too tired to exploit this mistake. He just stood there, panting.

The fight ended. Smith was awarded the unanimous decision, winning the UFC Heavyweight title in what was considered one of the biggest upsets in the UFC up to that point in time. The fight remains one of the most exciting in company history. Coleman's lack of cardio conditioning and overconfidence had destroyed him during the fight, especially coming up against Smith's superior conditioning and game plan.

"There are very few fights that I have ever seen that have torn me out of my seat," says Jeff Osborne. "This was one of the most memorable matches

I've seen live. There's a quote I used that Maurice asked if he could borrow, saying that 99 percent of fights hit the ground but 100 percent of fights start standing up."

Realistically, Smith's win over Coleman had very little to do with Smith's kickboxing skills. It was Smith's ability to hang on and play a good defensive game on the ground in the opening part of the fight, eventually getting Coleman to gas out, that won him the title. Smith simply played a smarter game. "Smith showed everyone that you did not have to be a submission expert to fight," says John McCarthy, who refereed the bout. "You really just needed to know how to defend yourself from one."

"It changed the course of what seemed to be a runaway train, in that ground fighters had dominated the UFC completely up until that point, with Gracie winning with jiu jitsu and Coleman and Severn winning with wrestling," says Stephen Quadros. "In people's minds back then it was perceived that ground fighting could not be beaten by standup fighting."

"Coleman was considered unbeatable," Quadros continues. "There is a scene in the Bruce Lee film titled *Return of the Dragon* where, after seeing Lee dispatch a bunch of thugs in a dark alley using his 'Chinese Boxing,' one of the workers at the restaurant that is being terrorized says in jubilation of Bruce's victory, 'Then we'll all give up karate' (which they had been training in to defend themselves). This, unfortunately, was still the mentality of most of those in or around the sport at the time Mo beat Coleman. People would change styles depending on who was winning at the time, as opposed to adding techniques to the ones they already had. So many, if not most, people flocked back to kickboxing, boxing, and Muay Thai schools. They had yet to realize that the hybrid athlete was soon to arrive, an athlete who had to know all styles, rather than just jumping from system to system depending on what was the flavor of the month."

If Coleman had not underestimated Smith and had proper conditioning for the fight, then, as in about 99 percent of wrestler versus kickboxer–type matches, Coleman probably would have won the fight. But that isn't what happened, and Smith had ended Coleman's reign as undefeated champion in the UFC. "Smith caught Mark Coleman at a time when everyone was thinking that Mark was unbeatable," says McCarthy. "Mark took the fight lightly and paid dearly for it. Not many people thought Smith had a chance against Mark."

"You can always speculate, but I feel I would've beaten him still [if Coleman had properly trained]," says Smith. "It would've been a harder fight, yes, but I would've won when he gassed out."

Smith didn't take any time off after the huge upset, and returned to defend his newly won championship at UFC 15 on October 17, 1997. His opponent was to be another highly skilled wrestler, Dan Severn. Again, it was a match Smith, still primarily a kickboxer, wasn't expected to win. Not only was Severn a great wrestler, but he also didn't have the cardio problems Coleman had, and he would be able to go the distance with Smith. On paper, it was a fight that Severn could have won.

But he didn't, because he didn't end up fighting. Days earlier, Severn had competed in the first PRIDE event in Japan. He went to a long and boring draw with Kimo, and injured his hand in the fight. He had to pull out of his title shot against Smith. UFC was fairly upset with Severn over the incident, and they only booked him once again, years later, as a last-minute replacement for another fighter. Smith versus Severn never happened.

On just a few days' notice, an out-of-shape and untrained Tank Abbott, weighing in at 277 pounds, took the bout. Ironically, he was the opponent PRIDE had originally sought for their debut show against Kimo, but he had trouble leaving the U.S. and getting into Japan, so Severn had taken his spot. Essentially, Severn and Tank had traded positions; Severn had fought Kimo in PRIDE, and Tank was now set to fight Maurice in UFC.

It was expected that Tank, being out of shape, wouldn't last long in the fight. Although Tank was competitive on his feet for a number of minutes,

Smith played another smart game, hanging back to let Tank tire himself out. When they ended up on the ground and did very little, referee John McCarthy restarted them. Smith started to tag Abbott with hard leg kicks, and Tank gave up before he could take any more punishment.

Since leaving Pancrase, Smith had gone undefeated in four fights, and had won both the Extreme Fighting and the UFC Heavyweight titles. He was the only fighter to ever hold both of those belts. He had been put through hard tests against Conan Silveira and Mark Coleman, and had seen impressive victories over Kazunari Murakami and Tank Abbott. When UFC held their first event in Japan on December 21, 1997, Smith was put to his next test, taking on highly skilled Greco-Roman wrestler–turned–mixed martial artist Randy Couture. This was the test that Smith wouldn't pass.

Ultimate Japan, headlined by Couture versus Smith for the UFC Heavyweight title, was held at the Yokohama Arena in front of 5,000 fans. Like Coleman, Couture was a world-class wrestler, but he wasn't going to gas out like Coleman had, and he wasn't going into his fight with Maurice without a game plan, like Coleman had. Couture took Smith down out of the gate, and moved right into side-mount, and most of the fight remained there, making the bout a somewhat dull affair. The fight ended up going to the judges, and they ruled in favor of Couture, giving Couture Smith's UFC Heavyweight title and the unanimous decision victory.

"When I fought Randy [Couture], it was a nice payday," says Smith. "After I fought, the pay dropped dramatically. I was really shocked, and I was upset, and I went elsewhere."

Smith returned to K-1, and took on former karate star and then–K-1 competitor Masaaki Satake in Japan. Smith went to a draw with Satake. Following that, Smith faced Ernesto Hoost in a rematch of their 1993 K-1 Grand Prix tournament fight, this time in the United States.

The fight took place on August 7, 1998. Smith took the kickboxing legend to the limit, and the fight went to the judges' table, where Smith lost a unanimous decision to Hoost. Smith fought once more in this run for K-1, against Mike Bernardo in the qualifier event on September 27 for the 1998 K-1 Grand Prix tournament in Japan. There Smith lost again via unanimous decision.

By the time Smith returned to the UFC octagon, having been unable to pick up a win in K-1, it was well over a year since his loss of the UFC Heavyweight title to Randy Couture at Ultimate Japan. Couture had since left the promotion in a contract dispute, and the Heavyweight title was vacant for the first—but not the last—time in its history.

Smith's first opponent back was Mark Coleman's protégé and training partner, Kevin Randleman, a former two-time NCAA Division I amateur wrestling champion whose natural athletic ability was freakily amazing. This was Randleman's UFC debut (he had competed in MMA elsewhere before, but this was his highest-profile fight up to that point in time), and the pairing of the novice against the veteran kickboxer who had defeated Coleman, Randleman's friend and training partner, made for an interesting matchup.

The fight took place at UFC 19, "Young Guns," on March 5, 1999. Odds were that Randleman wouldn't gas out like Coleman had, and this proved true indeed, as Smith and Randleman battled to the fifteen-minute time limit in a fairly slow bout fought largely on the ground. Smith made some submissions attempts, but Randleman was able to power out of them. The fight went to the judges' table. Smith again lost a clear unanimous decision. As the debuting Randleman had defeated the veteran Smith on a card called "Young Guns," it looked like Smith had passed the torch on to a newer generation of mixed martial arts fighters.

Smith's next opponent in UFC wasn't a young fighter like Randleman, however. At UFC 21 on July 16, 1999, he took on Brazilian vale tudo legend Marco Ruas. Like Smith, Ruas had hit his true athletic peak in the 1980s, and had made a name for himself as a top fighter while competing in vale tudo fights in Brazil throughout that decade. MMA had been around for decades in Brazil, under the name vale tudo, and Ruas was one of the top fighters to come out of that country's fighting system. He made his UFC debut in his thirties, at UFC 7 in September 1995, where he won the eight-man tournament. He had also competed in the 1995 Ultimate Ultimate, and lost a second-round decision to Oleg Taktarov. He had also continued to fight back in Brazil. Ruas's background was in Muay Thai, and thus this was expected to be an interesting standup and striking battle between two veterans of the ring.

Both men had something to prove, as both were clearly aging past their athletic peaks. Smith was coming off of his decision loss to Randleman at UFC 19. Ruas's last fight prior to this bout had been a bad loss nearly a year earlier at PRIDE 2 in Japan, where he fought lowly and then-inexperienced fighter Alexander Otsuka while he was sick. When he gassed out, Otsuka got the upset and defeated Ruas. Neither of them would take this fight lightly.

Smith ended up on top in this fight. Going in, Ruas had an injury that was fully healed, but it was reaggravated in the bout, so Ruas's corner threw in the towel at the end of the first round, giving the fight to Smith.

It would again be Smith's last UFC fight for a period, although this time he left the promotion on a win. He returned to Japan, where he fought in his debut fight with PRIDE. It was his only fight in that company during his career.

In PRIDE, he took on Branco Cikatic, another kickboxer who, ironically, had won the 1993 K-1 Grand Prix tournament in which Smith had made his K-1 debut. Under MMA rules, Smith was favored to win. He had experience in MMA in Pancrase, and at a high level in UFC, whereas Cikatic didn't have nearly as much experience with MMA rules under his belt.

The fight took place at PRIDE 7 on September 12, 1999. It was a slow fight, in which Cikatic received two yellow cards for grabbing the ropes. Smith managed to win the bout when he submitted Cikatic with a rudimentary forearm choke. It wasn't the striking war between two quality kickboxers that you might imagine. Not only was this the only fight of Smith's career in PRIDE, but it was also the only MMA fight that Smith would ever win via submission. It was also the last win in Smith's career that didn't go to a decision.

Less than a month later, Smith fought in MMA in the United States again, this time in a rematch against his old rival from Extreme Fighting, Conan Silveira. After having lost to Smith in Extreme Fighting in 1996, Silveira, who had once showed great promise, didn't really do anything with his career. He lost to Kazushi Sakuraba in his only UFC appearance at Ultimate Japan in 1997—the same card on which Smith lost his UFC Heavyweight title to Randy Couture. Silveira hadn't done much else of note in MMA since then.

Smith ended up losing to Silveira in their rematch, submitted with a choke from an on-top position at 2:48 of the second round. Smith the kickboxer had knocked out Silveira the jiu jitsu player years earlier in Extreme Fighting, and now Silveira had submitted Smith. It appeared Smith's career had come full circle.

But Smith kept fighting well past the age of forty. In December 1999, he fought in a tournament for RINGS, and defeated Branden Lee Hinkle (another training partner of Mark Coleman's) via majority decision in the first round before being submitted in less than a minute by Renzo Gracie in the second round.

"I was surprised at how fast Renzo was when he took me down," said Smith in an interview with Sherdog.com. "I think if I was fighting another person that was my size, as far as height, the same move wouldn't have happened. Being that he was short, he was able to get good position and then I was like 'damn, what am I doing here?'"

Smith also fought twice more in the UFC, first at UFC 27 on September 22, 2000, winning against Bobby Hoffman via decision in a standup fight in which Hoffman tired out early. "After my fight with Bobby [Hoffman], I look at the video and think I definitely won, but it could have been more decisive," Smith tells Sherdog.com. "People think he won because he sat on top of me and controlled me, but that's not a whole fight. I'm not really worried about knocking somebody out, I just want to win. I want to go to the third or fourth round, so I can see what someone has."

Smith's next fight was a loss via decision against then up-and-coming Renato "Babalu" Sobral at the very next UFC event on November 17, 2000. This loss to Sobral was Smith's last fight in UFC.

Smith continued to compete in K-1, right up to a U.S. pay-per-view televised tournament in May of 2001. In an exciting and climactic finish, he defeated Canadian fighter Michael McDonald in the finals to become K-1's USA tournament champion. Winning this tournament put Smith in the August 2001 K-1 qualifier, known as the Las Vegas Grand Prix tournament. There Smith went up against an up-and-coming Swedish fighter named Jorgen Kruth in the first round. Smith got past Kruth by winning a decision, but he then lost a close decision to his nemesis from Holland, Peter Aerts, the first and only fighter who had ever knocked him out cold.

Smith considered defeating Aerts to be more important than winning the tournament itself. It was a fight that Maurice had waited seven years for. It was a very exciting fight, and at the end of the three rounds, Maurice felt comfortable that he had won the decision, but the judges called the fight a draw. They went one more round for a tiebreaker, but Maurice had spent considerable energy in the first three rounds, and the overtime took a lot out of him. For the first time in ages, Maurice's conditioning was suspect, as Aerts controlled the overtime round.

Smith spent some time away from K-1, and two years later, he returned to fight in the 2003 K-1 U.S. qualifier tournament, which included K-1 veterans Michael McDonald and Rick Roufus, along with up-and-comer Carter Williams, among others. This was Smith's last tournament. He defeated Giuseppe DeNatale via decision in the first round before losing a decision to another American legend, Rick "The Jet" Roufus, in the second round.

Since 2000, Smith has fought in eight K-1 bouts, posting a record of 6–2, including a win over highly regarded Michael McDonald in May 2001 via split-decision—excellent for someone now in his mid-forties who has been competing in kickboxing bouts for twenty-five years.

Smith now trains many of today's top mixed martial artists and kickboxers in striking, including Randy Couture and Bob Sapp, Tsuyoshi Kohsaka, Allan Goes, Pete Williams, Frank Shamrock, Caol Uno, and many others. "I'll probably continue to do another year or two [of training other fighters]," says Smith. "I'm pretty accepting of the fact that I'm retired."

Smith was a kickboxer able to defeat a highly regarded jiu jitsu fighter and a highly regarded wrestler at a time when it was thought to be impossible for a kickboxer to do both. And that is the essence of his contribution to mixed martial arts. "You've got to have the smarts to know this game," Smith tells Sherdog.com. "Not anybody can come in here and do this. I don't know about IQ, but you've got to have the ability to learn, and then apply it. That takes some smarts, you know? Any of the top guys now are smart enough to improve their skills."

But, ironically, Smith's kickboxing skills didn't win those fights against Silveira and Coleman. Although he knocked Silveira out, Smith ultimately won because he went into both of those fights with a strong and very intelligent game plan and superior cardiovascular conditioning (as compared to Mark Coleman's lack of cardio in their fight) from his training with Frank Shamrock, and he had improved his ground game to the point that he could defend himself in a quality manner on the ground in those bouts. Smith helped open everyone's eyes to the fact that, if you want to succeed in this sport, then you must cross-train and have great cardio conditioning.

That is Maurice Smith's legacy in MMA.

Tito Ortiz

A tanned musculature, a bleached-blonde head, and a cocky attitude: this fighter's name hardly needs to be mentioned, as with this description, the "Huntington Beach Bad Boy" is instantly recognizable to mixed martial arts fans around the planet. Of course, this is Tito Ortiz, one of the most dominating champions in UFC history and arguably the biggest star created in UFC under Zuffa's management.

Born Jacob Ortiz on January 23, 1975, he was raised in Huntington Beach, California. He was a little troublemaker, leading his father to give him the nickname "Tito" when he was just two years old. Ortiz grew up on mean streets, and hung out with gangs, but in high school he turned his young life in a new direction by getting involved in sports. The young Ortiz was also a major pro wrestling fan, and this appreciation for sports entertainment later helped him evolve into a very charismatic personality for the UFC.

Ortiz began to wrestle in his sophomore year in high school, and he excelled at it. He continued in the sport at Golden West Junior College, where he tallied an undefeated record of 36–0 and became a two-time state champion. Ortiz was clearly a natural, and after high school he wrestled for Golden West Junior College in California.

Ortiz is actually a gifted athlete all around, and he soon discovered he was a natural at another sport when Tank Abbott, also from Huntington Beach and the original "Huntington Beach Bad Boy"—a nickname under which UFC would later market Ortiz—was looking for sparring partners in his hometown to prepare for his return to the octagon on September 20, 1996, at UFC 11, after a few months off. Ortiz ended up sparring with Tank.

Through connections made by sparring with Abbott, and after competing on a very small MMA show, Tito wound up in an alternates spot in the UFC 13 Lightweight tournament (called a "Lightweight" tournament even though many of the competitors were hovering around the 200-pound mark since UFC had only basic weight divisions at that time), on May 30, 1997.

"The first time I noticed [UFC] was Jerry Bohlander, when he won the first UFC lightweight tournament," says Ortiz in an interview for on-line magazine *SFUK*. "I saw that and I was like wow. I wrestled him in high school and I pretty much stomped him pretty easily, so I thought he does it well, so imagine what I could do. So at that time I just wanted to try and see how I would do."

As an alternate, Ortiz's fight wasn't part of the UFC 13 pay-per-view broadcast, but instead took place before the show went live on TV. His opponent was a guy named Wes Albritton, and in just thirty-one quick seconds, Ortiz took Albritton to the canvas and pounded him with strikes to end the match.

Of course, as an alternate, there was no guarantee that Ortiz would continue on in the one-night, four-man tournament. But, as luck would have it, Enson Inoue, having submitted Royce Alger earlier in the night in his first-round fight, pulled out of the tournament due to an injury. This gave Ortiz a chance in the finals, where he faced UFC veteran and then–King of Pancrase champion Guy Mezger, a trainee of the famed Lion's Den.

The fight against Mezger in the UFC 13 Lightweight tournament finals set off a long vendetta between Ortiz and the Lion's Den training camp, headed by Ken Shamrock. Tito was able to take Mezger to the ground early in the fight, and until the fight was stopped to check a cut Ortiz had opened on Mezger's head, he was ahead on points. However, instead of restarting the fight in the position it was stopped in, which would have been advantageous to Ortiz, it was restarted with both men on their feet. When Tito went to take Mezger down again, he made the rookie mistake of leaving his head out, and Mezger trapped him in a guillotine choke, forcing Ortiz to tap out.

"I trained for about four months with submissions before that," says Ortiz in an interview for *SFUK*. "I never knew what submissions were, so when he caught me in the guillotine I didn't know how to get out. I was inexperienced myself, I wish I had more time to train but you know I just fell into it just to give it a try and see how it was."

Due to the loophole in the UFC's rules regarding the position a fight is restarted in after the referee stops it to check a cut—a loophole that wouldn't be corrected until many years later—Tito was submitted in a bout that he had been winning up to that point. It cost him the tournament, but Ortiz would have a chance to avenge his loss against Mezger a couple of years later.

Ortiz took the Mezger fight as a lesson. He had made a simple mistake by leaving his head out for the choke, one that would be corrected with experience. Away from the UFC for some time after this, Ortiz competed in a small MMA show called the West Coast NHB Championships, where he pounded his opponent, Jeremy Screeton, into submission in only sixteen seconds.

Ortiz left the octagon temporarily in order to finish college at Cal State Bakersville. A little wiser and a little older, with three MMA fights under his belt, Ortiz made his comeback at UFC 18 on January 8, 1999, taking on another Lion's Den trainee, Jerry Bohlander.

At the time, Bohlander, like his training partner Guy Mezger, was a top fighter in the Light/Middleweight division of the UFC. Ortiz, on the other hand, was just a fighter who had shown some potential against the more experienced Mezger until he was submitted.

Ortiz was the dominant fighter in his bout against Bohlander, and had clearly improved since his last UFC outing. He was able to use his size and strength and wrestling skill to take Bohlander down and pound him, avoiding all submission attempts from the Lion's Den competitor. Ortiz ended up being too much for Bohlander, and the fight was stopped just into overtime due to a cut Ortiz had opened on Bohlander. After the fight Ortiz, always cocky in victory and willing to put on a show, put on a T-shirt that read "I Just

Fucked Your Ass." It was a bold statement, one that really announced that a new fighter was here to stay.

Ortiz had now defeated Mezger's training partner, and at UFC 19 on March 5, 1999, he returned to take on Mezger. In taking the rematch with Ortiz, Mezger had to give up the King of Pancrase championship because Pancrase didn't want their champion competing in another organization. The MMA world would soon find out whether or not Ortiz's loss to Mezger in the finals of the lightweight tournament at UFC 13 was a fluke.

Although Mezger was a more experienced kickboxer than Bohlander and was highly skilled in submissions, Ortiz used his strength and skill to put Mezger on the canvas and pound him while avoiding submissions. Ortiz had taken the fight on short notice and barely had over two weeks to seriously train.

The wait to see if any one of Mezger's submissions attempts would succeed on Ortiz like the guillotine choke had in their first fight was full of suspense, but just like in the Bohlander fight, Ortiz was too much. He was able to pound Mezger until he could take no more, and referee John McCarthy stepped in to stop the fight at 9:56.

In a span of a couple of months, Ortiz had gone from being a young fighter who showed some potential to being recognized as one of the best in the UFC's Middleweight division. To follow up the vulgar T-shirt he wore after defeating Bohlander, Ortiz put on a shirt after stopping Mezger that read "Gay Mezger Is My Bitch."

"Before that fight happened, he talked a lot of stuff. He said about the first fight that I was a young kid in a man's game and that his mom hits harder than me, he's thrown away more than I'll ever learn, and just disrespectful stuff like that," says Ortiz in an interview for *SFUK*. "I mean, I take that personally. So I thought about it. I thought, I'm making a T-shirt for this guy, he's kind of a pretty boy, his name's Guy Mezger, he's kind of like a gay guy, so hey, 'Gay Mezger Is My Bitch,' because I was going to make him my bitch that night. So when I beat him I strolled out and put the shirt on, I shot him down, it was like saying, 'Hey, you know what, you talk shit but now look who's on top.' Ken Shamrock got really mad. I mean, none of it was towards the Lion's Den or Ken Shamrock; everything was towards Guy Mezger. It's kind of bad when you put your foot in your mouth and can't pull it out."

Ironically, this shirt eventually led to one of the biggest money feuds in UFC after the turn of the century. On that day in 1999, Ken Shamrock, at ringside cornering Mezger and furious at the arrogant display of disrespect Ortiz had shown his fighter, got up onto the edge of the octagon and into Tito's face. In a famous clip (replayed a thousand and one times since), John McCarthy had to pull Tito away from Ken to avoid a brawl. Much later, toward the end of 2002, at the most-watched UFC pay-per-view in years, Ortiz would indeed have a brawl with Ken Shamrock.

But first, Ortiz had to fight a different Shamrock. Although Frank Shamrock had pretty much left UFC by that point in time, he called the promotion's head office to specifically request a fight against Ortiz. A cerebral athlete, and always looking for a new challenge, Shamrock saw Ortiz as the new wave of fighter, and he wanted to see how he'd fare against the newcomer. Shamrock also saw this as his chance to avenge the two losses his former training stable, the Lion's Den, had suffered at Ortiz's hands.

UFC jumped at the opportunity to take the fight, which was a smart move on their part. In the midst of the worst downturn in business in the UFC's short history, the fight went down as the most popular and influential match of the era.

Both Ortiz and Shamrock went into heavy training for the fight, which took place on September 24, 1999, at UFC 22. Shamrock was giving away about twenty pounds or so going in against Tito, and although he had defeated many larger fighters in many different ways throughout his career, he really hadn't faced anyone much larger and stronger than him with Tito Ortiz's brand of skill and ferocity. Shamrock put up his UFC Middleweight title (later to become the Light-Heavyweight title) in the contest.

It was a very exciting fight, and very brutal for both Ortiz and Shamrock. They fought into the fourth round, and Shamrock slowly fell behind on points. Just like he had against Bohlander and against Mezger in their rematch, Tito was able to use his size, strength, and wrestling skills to bully Shamrock and pound him. But in the fourth round, Tito learned a lesson that he'd never forget, as he simply ran out of gas. In a war of attrition, Shamrock held back, and took Tito's punishment, but because his cardio conditioning wasn't on Shamrock's level, Tito lost the war. At 4:42 of the fourth round, Ortiz gave up, and Shamrock got a come-from-behind victory. It was Shamrock's last fight in the UFC, and he retired a champion.

Ortiz took this defeat well, and proceeded to follow Shamrock's lead by becoming a total cardio machine. Tito made it clear that he would never gas out in a fight again.

Ortiz got his next chance to prove himself, this time against the very vicious and very dangerous Wanderlei Silva, a Brazilian fighter just starting out on a roll in PRIDE that would eventually lead him to become one of the greatest fighters the company had ever seen. Silva was vicious enough to have been nicknamed the "Brazilian Ax Murderer," and he certainly wore the label well, as he was a versatile fighter who could finish a fight in many ways. This bout, for the UFC Middleweight championship Frank Shamrock had vacated by retiring from UFC competition, took place in Japan at UFC 25 on April 14, 2000.

Overall, it was a long and slow fight, as Silva's main weapons, his soccer kicks and knees on the ground, are illegal in UFC. Without these tactics, Silva's offense wasn't at full capacity. Ortiz wrangled a decision victory out of Silva after going for five five-minute rounds. Although the fight was dull, the fact that Ortiz went the distance and won showed that he had definitely improved. Just one fight after gassing out and losing to Frank Shamrock, Ortiz demonstrated much-improved cardio conditioning, and the presence of a game plan by continuing to take Silva down and keep him on the mat.

The win over Silva earned Ortiz the UFC Middleweight title, and when that championship eventually became the UFC Light-Heavyweight title following Zuffa's purchase of UFC, Ortiz continued to dominate the division, defending the title against numerous very skilled challengers, and defeating them all—sometimes in very quick fashion—for many years.

The first challenger to his newly won belt was Japanese sensation Yuki Kondo, one of the best fighters to come out of the Pancrase system in that era. Kondo, a former King of Pancrase titleholder, had defeated Alexandre "Cafe" Dantas at UFC 27 to earn this title shot. The fight took place at UFC 29 on December 16, 2000, and although it looked like Kondo would be a real threat to Ortiz and his title, Ortiz was able to submit him in only 1:52 with a neck crank, the only time Ortiz has ever used a submission hold to finish an opponent.

Ortiz's next opponent was the formidable Evan Tanner. The fight against Tanner happened on February 23, 2001, at UFC 30, the very first event under the new ownership of Zuffa, the company that had purchased the promotion from SEG in January of 2001. Over the next couple of years, Tito would became a star.

The fact that Tito was on track to become such a big star had much to do with his charismatic personality and his unique look, combined with the fact that he was such a dominating fighter. He made quick work of the highly skilled Tanner, knocking him out with a huge slam in merely thirty-two seconds. Ortiz was beginning to look unbeatable. He followed up this impressive streak of quick and dominating victories by defeating the underrated Elvis Sinosic in only 3:32 at UFC 32 on June 29, 2001.

Tito's entire UFC run up to that point had been largely in obscurity as, although he was a superstar presence in the MMA world, UFC had only been available on pay-per-view to a very small number of homes since before Ortiz joined the promotion, having been axed by cable systems Viewer's Choice and Request (among others) years earlier. But under new management, the UFC would be reborn as a promotion, beginning with its debut on In-Demand pay-per-view with UFC 33, from the city of Las Vegas on September 28, 2001.

Of course, Tito was a natural choice to headline the event. His opponent was originally to be Vitor Belfort. Belfort was a fighter who had dominated the UFC years earlier until he ran into Randy Couture and experienced his first loss. Following the loss, Belfort saw his potential slowly wilt away. He wound up in PRIDE, and although he had some memorable fights and some memorable wins, he couldn't shake the aura of being a disappointment since he'd come on so strongly years earlier, when he was younger. Belfort saw a chance to redeem himself against Ortiz in what would have been a very difficult fight for the Light-Heavyweight champion (which Tito's Middleweight championship had morphed into months earlier).

Devastatingly, Belfort pulled out due to injury only a few days before the show. He had actually punched through a window and injured his triceps, taking thirty stitches. He had to be quickly replaced by Vladimir Matyushenko, who was originally supposed to fight Kevin Randleman on the event's undercard.

Matyushenko was a very dangerous opponent for Tito as, like Tito, he is a good wrestler. However, he went into the fight on just a few days' notice, and he had been training to fight Kevin Randleman, not Ortiz. The fight was long and dull, and Ortiz looked dominant as a wrestler, continually taking Matyushenko down to the ground and eventually winning a very easy unanimous decision victory.

As an event, UFC 33 was a major flop. A combination of factors, including the September 11th attacks earlier in the month and Belfort pulling out of the scheduled main event, among others, led the show to do roughly just 75,000 buys on pay-per-view, despite the fact that Zuffa had taken out heavy advertising for the show. Although it was the highest number of buys the UFC had done on pay-per-view in many years (since it was the first time they were available on most cable pay-per-view systems in a very long time), it fell far short of the record 250,000-plus buys that UFC had done for more than one event years earlier under the management of SEG.

The Ortiz-Belfort fight that never happened was rescheduled for UFC 36 on March 22, 2002, but bad luck struck again when Ortiz tore his ACL in training, and was put on the shelf for months. Due to Belfort's injury in 2001 and then the subsequent injury to Ortiz in 2002, Belfort versus Ortiz never happened, and will forever be a what-if in the annals of MMA history.

A bigger match was on the horizon for Ortiz and the UFC, though. Ken Shamrock had fought and lost a very close decision to Don Frye in PRIDE at the start of 2002. It was the final fight on Shamrock's contract with PRIDE, and because of the loss, his contract was not renewed. It was time for Shamrock to return to the UFC.

No one had forgotten the altercation after Tito had defeated Guy Mezger years earlier and donned the "Gay Mezger Is My Bitch" shirt—especially not Ken Shamrock. "Just because it was Guy Mezger, and [the shirt] said, 'Gay Mezger is My Bitch.' And Ken Shamrock disliked that a whole lot," says Ortiz in an interview with Mike Sloan for *UFC Fight News*. "He was very mad. I was just sticking up for myself, man. I'm in this game and I'm making a mark and if anybody tries to get in front of me, I'm just going to bulldoze right through 'em." Tito Ortiz versus Ken Shamrock was a fight that everyone had wanted to see. Appropriately subtitled "Vendetta," the event took place at UFC 40 on November 22, 2002, at the MGM Grand in Las Vegas.

Ortiz was clearly in another league than the veteran warrior, who was pounded on for three rounds. The fight ended when Shamrock, whose face looked like it had suffered a late-night encounter with a Mack truck, gave in after the third round ended.

"I've always respected Ken as a fighter," said Tito in his post-fight interview. "I've always looked up to him. As a person, we've had our differences. And today were squared away our differences in the octagon."

The win, and the exposure from it, were a huge boost to Ortiz's career. He had won a very one-sided fight over one of the biggest names in UFC history in Ken Shamrock. The show set a record live gate for UFC, and became the most-watched UFC pay-per-view under Zuffa's management with roughly 150,000 buys—a record that still stands today. The fact that this show did so well, whereas subsequent pay-per-views headlined by highly skilled but lesser-known fighters, like Matt Hughes, Sean Sherk, Frank Trigg, Chuck Liddell, and others, did roughly 60,000 buys or fewer (down to around 35,000 buys or so for UFC 42 with Sherk versus Hughes headlining in Florida), shows that the casual audience would sooner pay money to watch charismatic superstar personalities like Ken Shamrock and Ortiz beat the hell out of each other than watch excellent but far less charismatic competitors, like Sherk and Hughes.

"I just think I'm really brash, you know, I don't care about a lot of things any more," said Tito in an interview with *Boxing Insider* on his money-drawing charisma. "I'm a very dangerous fighter and I come out with ferocity. I come out with a good attitude of knowing that I'm going to beat my opponent. And I try to make sure that my fists do the talking, but I like to do a little bit of talking up the fight before. If that's what makes Tito Ortiz, I'm not going to be a guy who just lets my fight do the talking. I'll do a little smack-talking before. I'm just going to rule the octagon. In my mind, there's no one better than me. I've just got to make sure I work harder and harder each time I train. But when [they see] the Tito Ortiz who [fights back] in the octagon, people will know that's me, because there's no one in the world like me and there never will be anybody in the world like me. I just try to keep that persona in and out of the octagon, no matter what."

UFC 40 was extremely successful, aside for one flaw in Ortiz's post-fight interview. "I don't know. I'm not really thinking about that right now," said Tito when asked about the prospect of facing number-one contender Chuck Liddell. "Me and Chuck, I guess we gotta sit back and look at it. I guess we gotta renegotiate things, 'cause our friendship is not worth the money we're getting paid, if you ask me. I love Chuck as a friend. If we're gonna get in here and do what [Ken Shamrock and I] did right now, I'm gonna make it worth the while for myself and his self. So, I don't know, I guess we'll be going to Japan to fight possibly, but that's the last thing on my mind right now."

This interview seemed like a very small flaw at the time of the show. But Ortiz's failure to commit to the Liddell fight would in fact be the biggest story to come out of the UFC for months. After hammering Shamrock, Ortiz was easily the top star in the promotion, but he delayed the fight against Liddell (which was supposed to happen early in 2003) with numerous excuses, from contract issues to outside acting entertainment deals, minor surgery, and beyond. Whether or not these excuses were legit only Ortiz knows, but Liddell and Ortiz had been training partners years earlier, and in their sessions together, Liddell had handled Ortiz.

The situation grew bad enough that at one point, in the middle of 2003, it looked as though Tito wouldn't return to the UFC, and the promotion decided to create an interim Light-Heavyweight title. This title was put up for grabs between Chuck Liddell and former UFC Heavyweight champion Randy Couture (cut down to the Light-Heavyweight division for the fight), whom many saw as washed up after having lost his last two fights at the Heavyweight division.

Couture versus Liddell took place at UFC 43, and in one of the biggest upsets in company history, Couture defeated Liddell in a completely one-sided fight, winning the interim Light-Heavyweight championship.

With Couture as champion and Liddell seemingly out of the picture for the moment, Ortiz returned. Although the timing of the return was peculiar, considering that Liddell had just been knocked out of his number-one contender's spot, Ortiz claimed that his return had nothing to do with that, and that he had never ducked Liddell.

Ortiz sought to silence all skeptics by taking on Randy Couture to unify the two versions of the UFC Light-Heavyweight title at UFC 44 on September

26, 2003. The backstory for the fight was that Ortiz had never been put on his back in MMA competition because of his combined size and strength, and because he's a really good wrestler. Couture, on the other hand, was one of the best wrestlers in mixed martial arts at the time of the fight, although he hovered around age forty. Ortiz had lost a lot of respect from the MMA community for not taking on Liddell, regardless of whatever reasons he had for not fighting.

Ortiz clearly thought he could out-wrestle Couture, and Couture hoped to prove him wrong. Before a very packed house at Mandalay Bay in Las Vegas, Couture did just that, putting Ortiz flat on his back not only in the first round of the fight, but in every round thereafter, performing a suplex near the end of the last round. Ortiz seemed to be waiting for Couture to tire out, but despite his advanced age, Couture dominated the fight round after round and won a one-sided decision. Capping the bout, in the closing seconds of the fifth round, Couture stood over Ortiz, who was lying crooked on the canvas, and spanked him.

Crying after the fight, but gracious in defeat, Ortiz placed the Light-Heavyweight strap around Couture. It was Ortiz's first loss since his fight against Frank Shamrock back in 1999, and it was the first time in his mixed martial arts career that he had been so badly dominated by his opponent. "On that night, it was Randy Couture's night," said Ortiz in an interview with *MMA Weekly Radio*. "He fought a great fight and fought like a true champion. You know what, I thought I was ready, and I lacked the wrestling skills that he had, man. He had some of the best wrestling skills that I thought I would never see, and I did see them that night." The fight was simply a case of Ortiz mistakenly believing he could out-wrestle Couture, and although he had trained hard on his back in preparation for this fight, it may have been a case of overconfidence. "It just seemed like everything just wasn't clicking, man," says Ortiz on the loss. "It just seemed like I was a step behind him each and every step. . . . It was just, like, I was getting taken down. It wasn't really, in my mind, it wasn't like, 'Wow, I got taken down—oh no.' I expected to get taken down, but to get controlled as much as I did, I just felt like it wasn't my night. When he was shooting in on me and I couldn't stop his takedown, I was like, what's going on? I usually stop people's takedowns. Then I just kinda realized that my legs are a little too flat. I didn't have the speed and explosion that I usually have."

Drawing roughly 80,000 buys on pay-per-view, the show was a success for UFC. This made it the second most-watched UFC pay-per-view under Zuffa's management, although it fell way short of their record 150,000 buys for UFC 40. This gave Ortiz the distinction of having headlined the three most-watched pay-per-views under Zuffa: UFC 40 (150,000 buys), UFC 44 (80,000 buys), and UFC 33 (75,000 buys), easily making him the biggest star created by Zuffa.

As a fighter, Ortiz had greatly improved after losing to Guy Mezger, and he took this improvement to a whole new level after losing to Frank Shamrock. Logically, then, Tito should have been able to take his loss to Couture in stride and improve even further as an athlete. Unfortunately for him, though, his next opponent was an old demon coming back to haunt him. A demon named Chuck Liddell.

After losing to Couture in June 2003, Liddell competed in the PRIDE Grand Prix tournament, and after defeating Alistair Overeem in the first round, he was defeated by Quinton Jackson in the second in a one-sided fight. Ortiz versus Liddell was an interesting proposition for both fighters, as a year earlier they had arguably been considered the two best fighters at the light-heavyweight level on the planet: Ortiz was the UFC Light-Heavyweight champion, and Liddell was his number-one contender. But just a year later, Liddell had lost two of his three latest fights, and Ortiz had badly lost his only bout of 2003.

Both men were looking for redemption. The winner of this fight would have another shot at the Light-Heavyweight championship later in 2004, and the loser would move to the bottom of the division's ladder and have to work his way back to the top. Neither man wanted to be at the bottom looking up. "The reason I never fought Chuck Liddell before was because I thought he was a friend of mine," Ortiz told *Boxing Insider* before stepping into the octagon against Liddell. "But I guess, when money comes down to it, he doesn't care about friendship. He says that we never were good friends. So, that's even better. When I beat him down worse I don't have to think I beat down a good friend."

The fight took place on April 2, 2004, at UFC 47, aptly titled "It's On!" The long-awaited finish to one of the longest and most-discussed feuds in mixed martial arts history drew a tremendous gate at Mandalay Bay in Las Vegas, the second highest in company history behind UFC 40 at MGM Grand.

The first round of the fight was uneventful. Ortiz and Liddell danced, as Ortiz was clearly very cautious about mixing it up on his feet with Liddell, and rightfully so, considering Liddell's reputation as a dangerous striker. After a slow first round, going into the second it appeared that fans would see a disappointing fight go to a draw. But that's not what happened. Not a minute into the second round, Liddell managed to light Ortiz up and back him up against the fence. With a series of punches, Liddell put Ortiz to sleep, and that was all she wrote. It was over at thirty-eight seconds of the second round. With the win, Liddell earned himself another shot at the Light-Heavyweight title down the line and proved Tito's critics right.

It was a bad loss for Ortiz, who had never lost twice in a row, let alone been dominated twice in a row by his opponents. Close to the age of thirty, Ortiz still has many years left ahead of him in the sport—if he wants to keep fighting. "I'm not just going to be a fighter for the rest of my life," Ortiz tells *Boxing Insider*. "I'm trying to get something out so I'm not fighting until I'm forty years old. So I'm doing other things, like getting into movies. That's something I really think I can accomplish in my life."

Tito will get every chance to prove once more why he is the biggest star the UFC has produced since the promotion's mid-'90s boom period, and why he remains one of the top light-heavyweight fighters in mixed martial arts today.

Dan Severn

Most MMA combatants fight only three to four times per year at most, because of the tremendous toll the sport puts on an athlete's body. In 2003, Dan "The Beast" Severn fought in seven fights across the United States. Only a very slim percentage of fighters can take the punishment of MMA and continue to fight that often. But that's not the amazing part. Of those seven fights—two of which were eight days apart from each other and two of which were headline fights on King of the Cage pay-per-view events—Severn lost only one, via decision. But even that's not the amazing part. The truly amazing part is that Dan Severn was able to accomplish all of this at the age of forty-five—in a sport where most fighters are considered washed-up by their late thirties.

In addition to these seven fights, Severn was also involved in the independent pro wrestling scene, which is very taxing on an athlete's body. But coming from an amateur wrestling background, toughness and discipline are second nature to Severn.

"I was one of eight children," said Severn in an interview conducted for this book. "I was the second oldest. So my brothers started wrestling, and I played three sports: football in the fall, wrestling in the winter, and track in the spring. I did well in football. I had a number of full athletic scholarships. I had scholarships if I wanted to go and do track."

Severn considers his start in amateur wrestling as somewhat a fluke. "My first exposure (to wrestling) was in seventh grade," Severn says. "We didn't have youth programs back then like they do now. You can start wrestling at four years of age now in Michigan. Junior high school was my first exposure, in phys. ed. class where everyone had to participate. There was a gym coach who was all-in-one purpose. He was the wrestling coach, the basketball coach, all of that. We had games with the other schools, but it was limited. A flu epidemic had hit the school at the time, and a lot of people were out, and they asked me to sign up to a sport. I thought I'd try this thing called wrestling. And the following year I signed up for wrestling rather than basketball."

Severn started off slowly, but excelled as he gained experience. "I eventually had a lot of success in wrestling, but only through the principles of hard work and application."

Severn's wrestling successes included gold medals at the 1977 World Championship, the 1986 Pan-Am Championship, and the 1986 World Cup, and thirteen National AAU championships. Severn was also inducted into the wrestling Hall of Fame at Arizona State University, where he studied. "A lot of people don't know this about me," says Severn, "but I've got a bachelor of arts from Arizona State University. I am a certified secondary education teacher. I can teach on a high-school level.

"One of the things that sticks in the back of my mind is my amateur wrestling career," Severn continues. "I mean, I was a three-time All American, but I was never an NCAA champion. I was a runner-up, [and that] was as close as I came to it. Well, it makes you wonder what if I would've took that full athletic scholarship at Iowa University, would I have become NCAA champ then, but would I even be here today doing this?"

Severn competed on the amateur wrestling scene for most of his life, until one day a friend approached him with a tape of an event that had aired on pay-per-view. It was the Ultimate Fighting Championship.

"I lived out of Coldwater since 1992, and Coldwater did not have pay-per-view capabilities back then," remembers Severn. "A friend of mine out of Detroit videotaped and showed [the UFC events] to me. I said, 'Pretty intense, but I don't kick or strike.' My friend said to look at this jiu jitsu guy, Royce Gracie. I said, 'It kind of looks like wrestling,' but I didn't have any submissions.

"I filled out an application, and it listed all of the martial arts and to check off one," Severn continues. "'Wrestler' wasn't on there, so I wrote that down. They also asked about black belts. I didn't get a callback from submitting the application. They received something like two to three hundred applications a day."

Severn's manager for his pro wrestling gigs, Phyllis Lee, made a call to UFC promoter Art Davie about getting Dan into the next UFC tournament, and Davie agreed to come to a pro wrestling show to watch Dan in action.

"I wasn't supposed to be on the original card on UFC 4," says Severn. "Someone must've got hurt, I don't know the particulars, but they gave me a phone call. By the time I got the call, I had five days to prepare for my match and go out there and compete."

Severn trained with pro wrestler and martial arts trainer Al Snow, who had a makeshift wrestling school in Lima, Ohio. "It was five days of training that was kind of a joke," says Severn. "It was held in Lima with Al Snow and two other pro wrestling protégés. They put boxing gloves on, and the name of the game was 'Punch Dan.'"

Severn made his debut in the first round of the UFC 4: Revenge of the Warriors tournament, becoming the first former amateur wrestler to make a big name for himself in MMA, an astounding and highly influential feat, considering the enormous number of amateur wrestlers who would follow him into the sport after this point. Many of these wrestlers would have fantastic success, as the technique and discipline of amateur wrestling seem to adapt well to MMA.

"My guarantee walking out there was $1,000," says Severn. "I'd never worked on strikes and submissions, so I walked out there basically a pure amateur wrestler." He continues, "By contract, as long as I finished in the top two people, I get to come back again. Well, I was a last man [in the tournament]."

In the first round, Severn went up against Anthony Macias, and during the fight, two highlight reel moments occurred when Severn suplexed Macias over his head twice in a row. "The UFC had never seen anyone picked up bodily and being launched around," remembers Severn. "While my background is freestyle wrestling, [that was] Greco-Roman. The guy was in position and threw a couple of elbows that hit me on the head, and I just went into autopilot. I arched up and bang! Launched him onto his head and shoulders. He came back up again, and I threw him even harder yet, and he hit so hard his own knee actually came up and split his eyebrow open. That's the kind of impact that he hit with."

Severn finished Macias off with a choke, and moved on into the second round to fight Marcus Bossett. He choked Bossett out less than a minute into the fight, putting himself in the tournament finals. The fighter on the other side of the octagon for the final fight of the night was then-two-time UFC tournament champion, Royce Gracie.

Gracie, the UFC's biggest name, was considered to be the best fighter on the planet at that time. He had developed a reputation for being able to easily defeat fighters much larger than him. Dan Severn definitely fit that description, as he was about seventy pounds heavier than Gracie. And although Severn was a talented freestyle wrestler, he had come into the UFC with only five days of training, and he didn't know what to expect out of the fights. Gracie had already won two tournaments and had loads of experience in the sport.

Severn took Gracie down and kept him there for the entire fight. Severn's lack of experience in the sport and his unwillingness to strike his opponent cost him in this fight, though. "I was struggling more with my conscience than I was with Royce," he reveals, adding, "even only after a few minutes, I struck Royce."

The fight continued for over fifteen minutes, until Gracie finished Severn with a triangle choke and won the tournament. "Was [the loss] because someone beat me, or was it because I wouldn't do something to someone?" says Severn on Royce's victory.

"Being out there, striking is not my forte," Severn continues. "It's something that I had to acquire, and I kind of feel bad when I have to utilize it. It's not the right frame of mind to have, being in this type of competition, but nevertheless, I still feel bad when I have to utilize it."

Severn may have been defeated by Royce, but a new respect for both Severn and amateur wrestling was born, as he had been able to do what only very few fighters on the planet have done in taking Gracie to his limit. Many experts firmly believe that if Severn had more MMA experience at the time he fought Gracie, or if Gracie had accepted a rematch (which Severn lobbied for later in his UFC career), then Severn would have defeated Royce. Chalk it up to experience. "If Royce had to face me after my training camp [before UFC 5], it would have been tough," says Severn. "I'm not going to predict the outcome, but. . . . "

Severn returned to the UFC for their fifth event, held in April 1995, and dubbed "Return of the Beast" after Severn. "I had a thirty- to thirty-two-day block of time," says Severn on his training time for UFC 5. "I had two training camps I set up in Arizona, away from my family so I could get the best results. I watched videotapes. It was always something: cardio, training all the time. I trained to strike. I looked at what the rules were so I could come up with ideas. I'm a competitor."

Severn defeated Joe Charles in the first round of the UFC 5 tournament in Charlotte, North Carolina, and met up with top Russian fighter Oleg Taktarov in the second round. Severn ended the fight by getting on top of Taktarov and kneeing him until he opened up a vicious cut on the Russian's face, and the referee stopped the onslaught. This put Severn in the finals. The Beast was unleashed.

Severn's nickname, "The Beast," was actually coined by legendary football player and former UFC broadcaster Jim Brown. "To have such an endorsement from one of the most punishing running backs in the history of the game, that's quite a feather in my hat," says Severn on his nickname. "He called me a Dr. Jekyll and Mr. Hyde." Severn has always been known for his contrasting character: he's a tough-as-nails competitor in the ring, but most will concede that he's a gentleman away from it. "I can only speak for myself," says Severn on the crude behavior of some fighters outside the ring. "[Being a gentleman] is the way I will conduct myself, but tough and crazy does sell tickets."

Severn's opponent in the UFC 5 tournament finals was Canadian fighter Dave Beneteau. Severn defeated him with a keylock submission to win his first UFC tournament championship. Severn proved to the world that he belonged in UFC's top tier of fighters by mustering up his competitive nature to come back from defeat at Gracie's hands and win the UFC 5 tournament. "I do not call myself a fighter. I'm a competitor," says Severn. "I'm competitive if I'm playing checkers. It's my nature."

UFC 5 was an extremely successful event for UFC. Alongside the tournament, dominated by Severn, the main event of UFC 5 was a special "Superfight" challenge match between Ken Shamrock and Royce Gracie, for the newly created UFC Superfight championship belt (which later evolved into the UFC Heavyweight title). It was Gracie's final fight in UFC, and it ended up going to a time-limit draw. UFC 5 was the most-watched pay-per-view in company history up to that point in time.

Well, that record didn't hold for long, as UFC 6: Clash of the Titans, in July 1995, garnered an even higher pay-per-view buyrate. To this day, UFC 6 remains the most-watched UFC event of all time. And the main event, you might ask? It was Ken Shamrock against Dan Severn in a special challenge match for the UFC Superfight title, still vacant after Shamrock and Royce Gracie had fought to a draw.

Severn, with his considerable size advantage over Shamrock and his wrestling proficiency—along with the fact that he had improved a great deal in striking and finishing fights since his UFC debut—was favored to defeat Shamrock and win the championship belt. But that's not what happened in the end, as Shamrock upset Severn by submitting him with a guillotine choke just a little over two minutes into the fight, becoming the first-ever UFC Superfight champion.

"I was sick that night," recalls Severn. "I had strep throat and a 102-degree fever. I walked out there, but my competitive spirit was at home in bed. . . . Why did that fight ever take place in the first place? I didn't understand the thinking of it," Severn continues, with regard to his Superfight with Shamrock. "I thought to be in a superbout, people had to achieve a level of success. I'd won a tournament and been a runner-up in another. What had Ken really accomplished? He was never even a runner-up. I didn't understand this bout with Ken. You then had the Kimo versus Ken bout. Kimo never won a tournament then, and he never even won a match at that point. My mind's a little tainted from my amateur wrestling career, but I think you have to be a proven commodity."

The Shamrock versus Severn feud, which culminated in another encounter between the two at UFC 9: Motor City Madness, remains one of the most legendary feuds in MMA history. UFC pay-per-views rivaled major pro wrestling and boxing events in popularity and demand in the mid-1990s, and many attribute UFC's success in that era to Ken Shamrock, Royce Gracie, and Dan Severn—pillars of its popularity. And not only were they the fighters from that era whom people would pay to see, but they were also the best inside the octagon. "I don't know the guy," says Severn of Ken Shamrock. "The only time I ever shared with him, we were out in the octagon, and we weren't exactly exchanging pleasantries." Severn continues his thoughts on Shamrock by saying, "I'm not exactly a fan of Ken's. I don't have anything against the guy. I always say that actions speak louder than words, and if you ever watch his actions . . . he's not a person I care for."

At this point, UFC decided to do something exciting and drastic. They held a tournament between the top eight fighters in UFC to determine who was the number-one fighter on the planet. People wanted to know who the best-of-the-best was. They had to know. This demand gave birth to the Ultimate Ultimate tournament, held in December of 1995 in Denver, featuring eight of the most well-known fighters on the planet at the time: Dan Severn, Marco Ruas, Oleg Taktarov, Tank Abbott, Steve Jennum, Paul Varelans, Keith Hackney, and Dave Beneteau.

UFC received national publicity in the week leading into the show because the mayor of Denver moved the show from its original venue, but a compromise was reached, and the show was held in a smaller building, Mammoth Gardens, selling out to 2,800 fans. The show went head-to-head with a Mike Tyson fight on national TV, but the live showing still drew an amazing buyrate, and the replay directly afterward drew the largest buyrate in history for a replay of a pay-per-view event. The combined live showing and replay did the third biggest buyrate in UFC history, a record that stands to this day.

Severn's first-round opponent was the gigantic Paul Varelans, whom Severn submitted in less than two minutes. "Varelans was a big guy. Nice guy," says Dan. "I took him down and went for a hammer strike, but he blocked it. I just trapped his arm across his face and went for a choke and a neck crank."

Severn continued on into the second round against David "Tank" Abbott, and their fight went to the time limit. "Tank's a dangerous guy on his feet," recalls Severn. "I needed a clinch or a takedown. Once on the mat I had to stay busy because of the new non-activity clause, because I did not want it on our feet. I just punched in the time clock and went to work on him."

Severn captured the judges' decision in his fight against Abbott, and advanced to the finals. His opponent there was Oleg Taktarov, in a rematch from their fight at UFC 5. "Russians have a mind-set where you almost have to kill them. I'm not going to stop unless he's unconscious. I went in and did what I had to do," says Severn on his fight against Taktarov.

Taktarov did prove to be a more formidable opponent this time around, as the match went to a decision—Severn's second that night. And, just like the first fight, he won this decision as well, becoming the winner of the most important tournament up to that point in MMA history.

As the first Ultimate Ultimate tournament champion (a second Ultimate Ultimate tournament, won by Don Frye, was held in December 1996), Severn took home both tremendous respect and a tremendous purse: $150,000. In fact, it was the largest purse awarded in MMA history up to that point in time. Since the 1995 Ultimate Ultimate went down as the third most-watched UFC event in history, it put Dan Severn in a headline position in the three most-watched UFC pay-per-views of all time. "Although the Ultimate Ultimate belt is the smallest, it is the one I cherish the most," says Severn of the tournament victory. "The show was over two hours, and I fought three times. My matches represented roughly 50 percent of the show."

The Ultimate Ultimate tournament victory forced UFC to give Severn a rematch with UFC Superfight champion Ken Shamrock. UFC saw Severn as uncharismatic and no longer wanted him in a headline position. Fearful that he would defeat Ken Shamrock, their meal ticket on pay-per-view at the time, UFC had not wanted to put together the Shamrock versus Severn rematch. But because Severn had shown a tremendous amount of skill in the Ultimate Ultimate, they ultimately had no choice. "He was the golden boy," says Severn on the matter of the UFC protecting Ken Shamrock. "He had the look, the hard body. I was a monkey wrench in that system."

The rematch between Shamrock and Severn was set for UFC 9: Motor City Madness, in May 1996. By this point, outside political pressure due to the perceived violence of the sport was attempting to stifle UFC, and the number of homes that UFC shows were available in began to decrease due to a cable ban. In addition to this, the popularity of UFC as a whole was winding down, and the show did a disappointing buyrate on pay-per-view for that era. "UFC at first got over being a novelty," says Dave Meltzer, editor of the *Wrestling Observer*, on the topic. "Once people realized who would win between guys of certain disciplines, some of the UFC novelty was lost. In addition, UFC was hurt badly when Royce Gracie bowed out without losing. As well, Severn and Shamrock had fought once, and Shamrock won easily and quickly. I think there wasn't a lot of confidence that a second time would be different. I think a lot of things hurt business, and most of it was the cable ban."

The rematch itself between Shamrock and Severn was also a disappointment. Neither fighter was willing to engage the other, and they spent the entire fight dancing around each other with very little action. The fight, which featured roughly ninety seconds of action, went to a thirty-minute time-limit draw. "I knew that the crowd wasn't going to like this match," says Severn on the fight. "So when the crowd starts booing, how are you going to let 10,000 people affect you in your mind-set? And it did get to [Shamrock]. There was garbage being thrown in. John McCarthy stopped the match at one point in time and was yelling at us because we weren't engaging in a fight, and he was pushing us back and restarting us. It doesn't bother me at all. Things are working for me just fine."

Shamrock had already fought in two previous headline matches—against Royce Gracie and Oleg Taktarov—that slowly went to the time limit. Many viewers of those earlier contests saw Shamrock as the unofficial winner. But since there were no judges when Shamrock fought against Royce and Oleg, those fights simply ended in time-limit draws. "If you look at most of [Shamrock's] matches, he's a counter person," says Severn. "He counters things. He doesn't go on that much of the aggressiveness. And I thought if I just sit back there and mirror what he's going to do, it's going to be a pretty boring match."

At this point, the UFC had started to use ringside judges. Although the UFC wanted to protect Shamrock, on this occasion the judges' decision was to award Dan Severn the fight and the championship belt. Severn versus Shamrock II went down as one of the dullest and most loathed fights in MMA history.

"That fight hurt the marketability of Shamrock, Severn, and the UFC, because at the time they were the two big stars and they didn't fight," says Dave Meltzer. "Had it been in the old format of no time [limit], they would've ended up with a decisive winner," Severn says on the controversy. "I can understand why they would do that from a promotional perspective, because they only have so much airtime. I have mixed emotions on it."

Severn, now the UFC Superfight champion, took some time away from the UFC to compete in other events. In July of 1996, he fought at Vale Tudo Japan 1996, submitting Doug Murphy with a keylock just over three minutes into their fight. Severn also made his debut on an American independent MMA show on September 1, 1996, at Brawl at the Ballpark 1, where he managed to submit Dennis Reed with a neck crank. Later, after Severn's UFC career had ended, he would become a fixture on the independent MMA and pro wrestling scenes.

Severn also competed at an event in Brazil called Universal Vale Tudo Fighting 4 during his time away from UFC, and at the first Extreme Challenge event, held by an independent promotion that is still around to this day.

Severn made his return to UFC at UFC 12: Judgment Day, on February 7, 1997, for his first UFC Superfight title defense. Mark Coleman, another former amateur wrestler, had won gold medals at the 1990, 1991, and 1992 Pan-Am Championships, and placed seventh in freestyle wrestling at 100 kilograms at the '92 Olympics in Barcelona, and had dominated the UFC scene while Severn was away. Coleman had won two eight-men tournaments at UFC 10 and UFC 11, and was now up for a title shot against Severn.

Coleman ended up choking Severn out nearly three minutes into the fight to win the UFC Superfight title, which would soon be rechristened as the Heavyweight title. But Severn didn't stop to think about the loss, as just three months later, he was back to working independent dates. He did six more fights in the independent scene and in Brazil before PRIDE made its debut as a promotion on October 11, 1997. Severn was on the card for the first PRIDE event, where he took on the enigmatic Kimo Leopoldo. Kimo and Severn went to a very dull thirty-minute draw reminiscent of Severn's rematch with Ken Shamrock at UFC 9 in that neither fighter was willing to engage the other. It was Severn's only fight in PRIDE. "Severn never really clicked in Japan because they had already seen him in [pro wrestling company] UWFI, and he wasn't a top guy there," says Meltzer on Severn's lack of popularity in the land of the rising sun.

The fight against Kimo also damaged Dan's relationship with UFC. "He got on the wrong side of the [UFC] by taking the Kimo fight with PRIDE just days before a scheduled title fight with Maurice Smith that I'm almost sure he would have won," says Meltzer. "When he was all banged up after the Kimo fight, UFC was pissed at him for screwing up their main event." Tank Abbott ended up getting the title match against Smith, and Smith defeated him at 8:08 into the fight. This ended Severn's affiliation with UFC for over three years, and realistically ended his run as a top fighter on the national scene.

The fight against Kimo was Severn's last fight of 1997, but he picked up strongly in 1998, competing in a total of seven fights throughout the United States that year, including a draw with legendary fighter and trainer Pat Miletich at Extreme Challenge 20 in August. Severn continued to fight at a fast pace throughout 1999, taking and winning four fights, three of which were held at events put on by his own promotion, DangerZone. Topping off his independent MMA success in this era, Severn also had a run with the World Wrestling Federation in late 1998 and into the start of 1999.

Not only has Severn worked an incredible number of independent MMA and pro wrestling dates, but he also gives speeches and seminars throughout the U.S. and abroad. "I probably work for more small companies than anyone else," says Severn. "I'm still trying to help this sport grow and be understood the right way. When you think about fighting, can you think of anything positive? Me, I can't. I can't really think of anything positive. That's why I do lots of speaking engagements with youth groups, juvenile centers, high schools, and I promote education."

Severn started off the new millennium by taking on future UFC Heavyweight champion Josh Barnett at SuperBrawl 16. Severn was able to last with Barnett—who, at roughly half Severn's age, is considered one of the best heavyweight fighters on the current scene—until the fourth round, when Barnett submitted him with an armbar.

But Severn didn't stop there. He competed on the independent scene eight more times in 2000, and won all eight fights. "I enjoy competition," says Severn. "I have a lot of promotions that do contact me. This industry is moving forward, and I want to have influence on that."

Severn fought a total of nine independent fights in 2000, but this didn't keep him from making a return to UFC when the opportunity arose. Pedro Rizzo, one of the top heavyweights in MMA at that time, renowned for being a devastating striker, was supposed to fight at UFC 27: Ultimate Bad Boyz, but his opponent was injured before the event. "The person who was supposed to face Rizzo got hurt. I got less than two weeks' notice to come in," says Severn on the fight with Rizzo. "I called [former UFC promoter Bob Meyrowitz] and said I'd take the match. He asked, 'What kind of shape are you in?' I said I'd give him the best match a forty-two year old can give. Was I in the greatest of shape? No. But I wasn't going to get asked to come in otherwise."

The fight took place on September 22, 2000, and it didn't last long, as Rizzo's amazing striking power overcame Severn just a little over a minute into the fight with a brutal kick to the leg that effectively ended the fight. Although Severn had been defeated quickly, he retained his opponent's respect.

"I saw him the first time when he fought Royce Gracie at UFC 4. I saw him in UFC 5 and then in Ultimate Ultimate, beating all the guys. My biggest idol is Marco Ruas, and I thought Marco could beat him. But they never had the chance to fight against each other. And now someone called me after the Randleman fight and asked me if I would fight against Dan Severn. Dan is a legend, one of the greatest I have seen, but he was just one more competitor. I had to beat him. I had to beat him that time."

Severn didn't let up on the number of fights he competed in after this point, though, fighting in seven fights in 2001 alone, losing just once to Jonathon Wiezorek via choke in the second round of their fight on April 21, 2001. Although Severn had built a reputation in MMA for being someone who would take any fight at any time as long as the promotion booked him, over the course of his career that mentality damaged his drawing power as a fighter. "Dan fought so often on lower-level shows that seeing a Dan Severn fight wasn't as much of a big deal because they happened sometimes every weekend," says Meltzer. Nonetheless, the loss against Wiezorek was one of only seven losses in Severn's career.

Severn continued on with six fights in 2002—all of which he won—and seven fights in 2003, with one loss and two draws. "I gave myself to age forty-six," says Severn. "I still enjoy the competition, but eventually Father Time catches up to you. I'd rather retire on my terms . . . than [have] some young buck wreck me and retire me."

"For a fighter's rep, it's best to retire on top," says Meltzer. "For his pocketbook, in most cases, that doesn't work out, because they need the money, and it becomes a job. Nobody really likes to see a legendary fighter slide downhill, but, inevitably, that is going to happen to everyone because age is the great equalizer. A lot of the older fighters are banged up to the point they shouldn't be fighting, but need the money because they have a name and it's what they do."

Severn has been talking about retirement for the past few years, and this certainly isn't the first time that the question has been brought to his attention. "I've been told on more than one occasion to stop wrestling," says

Severn frankly. "They told me I had to stop wrestling back in the '76-'77 season due to injury." He continues, "I'll be involved in MMA as long as I can, maybe as an influence behind the scenes."

"I don't know in the long run if it would change history, but Severn was very important in getting over to people that wrestling is an awesome base for fighting," says Meltzer. "Severn never got the credit he deserved for the fact that so many kids in those years wanted to be amateur wrestlers because they believed it was a great skill for real fighting. In previous generations, people would have thought going to the martial arts dojo and learning kung fu would be more beneficial."

Severn remains interested in a return to UFC. "Why haven't they brought me back? I've contacted them several times," he notes. "They asked me to be at [the UFC Legends ceremony in 2003]. I talked to Dana White and said I would really rather compete."

There has always been something of a consensus in MMA that Severn doesn't have the qualities a promotion looks for in a true headline fighter. "I think there was a feeling he didn't have enough charisma to be a headliner, but because his wrestling was so strong, he could simply outwrestle a lot of people," says Meltzer. "There is also the paradox about MMA fans. They want to see who would win in a realistic situation, but they want it also to be a kickboxing match. If wrestling can physically dominate, they think it's a boring fight, and the emphasis is on exciting fights as opposed to proving who is the best."

"I'm one of the purest competitors ever," says Severn. "No ulterior motives. That was when I first began. I've been tainted over time. Every promotion I go to, they give me the microphone because I ask for it, as I want to address the supporters and fans of the sport and say thanks. There's no industry without them."

Severn may not have much time left in the sport, but he will be remembered and respected as a fighter who considered himself more of a gentlemanly competitor. The idea of a "gentleman" competing inside of MMA might seem ironic, but Severn proves the irony true.

"I wouldn't mind one more UFC. I wouldn't mind one more PRIDE match. If it happens, great, if it doesn't, shame on them is how I look at it," says Severn on the current MMA scene. "Now it's all the gloves, the rounds, the weight classes. More and more you can't do this, you can't do that, and on and on. I believe overall the athletes themselves . . . a lot of athletes were one-dimensional athletes [at the beginning], and I throw myself in that category. I was just an amateur wrestler. Now you have a very hybrid athlete that has transformed since that time. Now standup strikers are learning survival skills on the ground. The grapplers are learning survival skills on their feet. It's a great deal of cross-training that's taking place. I don't know if a lot of the one-dimensional athletes would do as well with today's competitors." An ironic quote from an ironic man.

Randy Couture 6

If you took all of Rocky Balboa's characteristics, like his never-say-die spirit and the idea of always being in the underdog position, and created a mixed martial artist based on that persona, you'd end up with Randy "The Natural" Couture. Like Rocky, Couture has made a career out of going into a fight as the underdog and coming out the victor. He never loses when popular opinion positions him as the underdog going into one of his fights, and more often than not, his fights would be worthy of being in a Rocky film. He was the first man to become a two-time UFC Heavyweight champion, and the first man in UFC history to win a championship title in two different weight divisions. He may be the most accomplished mixed martial artist of all time, and the fact that he's done most of this while hovering around the age of forty is simply incredible in itself.

Born on June 22, 1963, in Washington State, Couture is nearly a lifetime amateur wrestler. He started wrestling while he was in junior high school, and once he got into it he never looked back.

In high school, Couture won the Washington State Championship, fore-shadowing his later success in wrestling in the military and for Oklahoma State.

After graduating from high school and getting married at the age of eighteen, Couture joined the army and wrestled for All-Army. He also trained in boxing for a number of weeks while in the army, training that would prove useful years later when he competed in the UFC. Beyond his brief boxing stint, he spent most of his days in the army wrestling. "Basically all I did was wrestle for the service," says Couture. "My last three years in the military, I was assigned to the sports department, and wrestling was basically my job."

After six years of wrestling in the service, Couture felt it was time to leave the military. He wasn't interested in making a career as a soldier, and after training with the army for the 1988 Olympic trials, he left the army for college.

Couture was accepted into Oklahoma State University, where he—naturally—quickly excelled in wrestling. With Oklahoma, Couture ended up becoming a three-time NCAA Division I All-American, placing sixth in 1990 at 190 pounds, second in 1991, and then second again in 1992 in the same weight division. Couture also captured first place in the USA Senior Greco-Roman Championships in 1990 and 1993 at 198 pounds, and did the same years later in 1997 at the 213.8-pound division. Couture also placed first in the 1991 Pan American Championship for Greco-Roman wrestling at the ninety-kilogram level after coming in second in the same competition a year earlier. He was also an alternate for the U.S. Olympic team four times. Simply put, Randy Couture is an incredible Greco-Roman wrestler.

After graduating from university with a major in German, Couture watched a UFC event and saw Don Frye, whom he had known through the amateur wrestling grapevine, competing. Couture was interested in the idea of fighting in UFC, and he sent an application to SEG, but he was turned down because they weren't looking for amateur wrestlers at the time, having filled their wrestling quota with such names as Frye, Dan Severn, and Mark Coleman, among others.

Couture continued to compete in amateur wrestling, and was soon approached by a group of amateur wrestlers-turned-mixed martial artists, including Tom Erikson, Rico Chiaparelli, and Frank Trigg, who had formed Real American Wrestlers (RAW), a stable of amateur wrestlers training with each other for mixed martial arts competition. They asked Couture to join their team. "Having been friends of theirs through wrestling," says Couture, "I was one of the athletes they approached about being a member of RAW."

Couture soon had a chance to become a top fighter himself as, while he was competing in the 1997 Pan American Championship in San Juan, Puerto Rico, in late May (where he placed third in the ninety-seven-kilogram class in Greco-Roman wrestling), SEG asked him to fill in for another fighter who had been injured in the four-man UFC 13 Heavyweight tournament. Despite the fact that he only had a few weeks to train with his RAW contemporaries for the event, Couture jumped at the opportunity to compete in UFC.

UFC 13 took place on May 30, 1997, in Birmingham, Alabama, just days after the Pan American Championship in Puerto Rico. Couture's first-round opponent in the one-night tournament was Finnish boxer and wrestler Tony Halme, also making his UFC debut. Halme had been an upper-card pro wrestler for the WWF in the early 1990s under the name of Ludvig Borga, and he later became a politician in his native country. Couture went into the fight after barely one week of training with the RAW team in Atlanta.

Couture's debut fight in UFC was successful; he submitted Halme with a rear naked choke just under a minute into the fight. This advanced him into the second and final round of the tournament, where he successfully stopped Steven Graham at 3:13. With that win, Couture, pretty much a pure Greco-Roman wrestler at the time, won the four-man UFC 13 Heavyweight tournament and procured a successful UFC debut. It was the start of a long-standing legacy in UFC.

With a couple of fights' worth of experience under his belt, Couture returned to UFC 15 on October 17, 1997, where he took on Vitor Belfort. Belfort, a young Brazilian Jiu Jitsu master, had been labeled a phenomenon, and was undefeated at that point with what many felt were the fastest hands UFC had ever seen. Belfort was a highly skilled grappler, but more often than not, he used his fast hands, not his grappling skills, to quickly eliminate his opponents.

So far, Couture's only experiences in UFC were his two wins over opponents considered to be tomato cans in the UFC 13 Heavyweight tournament, and Belfort was the newest, deadliest rising star in UFC at that point. Most figured that, although Couture had won the UFC 13 Heavyweight tournament, he stood little chance against Belfort.

Couture proved doubters wrong, however, in his fight against Belfort, using his Greco-Roman wrestling skills to tie his opponent up in a clinch and prevent him from striking. Couture also showed skill with very accurate punches of his own from within the clinch. Another issue that worked to Couture's advantage was that, before the fight, Belfort claimed he had a stomach virus. It was hard to get Belfort out of his trailer that night, and he looked sluggish during the bout.

Couture ended up out-striking Belfort on their feet, and a few minutes into the fight, Belfort gassed. Couture did a number on him until referee John McCarthy stopped the fight. Couture had just stopped the deadly rising star in his tracks and, in the process, made a real name for himself in UFC.

It wasn't the last time Couture went into a fight the underdog and destroyed a rising star. The win earned Couture a title shot at the UFC's then-reigning Heavyweight champion, Maurice Smith, at UFC's first Ultimate Japan event held in Yokohama on December 21, 1997. Smith had scored a huge upset victory at a prior event against another wrestler, Mark Coleman, to win the belt.

The fight was a long, slow bout. Couture was able to avoid Smith's kickboxing skills and get him up against the fence for a takedown. Both fighters remained on the ground for the rest of the regulation period.

At the start of the first overtime period of the fight, Couture again took Smith down, and kept him there. The same thing happened in the second overtime of the fight, as Couture slowly grounded and pounded Smith throughout the entire match. It went to the judges' table, and Couture was awarded the unanimous decision victory and the UFC Heavyweight championship, the first time he would wear that belt.

After appearing in just three UFC events and taking on only four opponents, the undefeated Randy Couture had risen to the top of the UFC Heavyweight division and captured the UFC Heavyweight championship. Couture was now on the road to becoming one of the most decorated fighters in mixed martial arts history. Unfortunately, he entered UFC at a bad time in the promotion's history, as the cable ban had taken effect just before Couture's debut with the company at UFC 13, and they were losing money. A situation cropped up, and UFC told Couture they were unable to pay him what was designated in his original contract. "They had signed me to a three fight deal," said Couture in the book *Brawl*, "with a certain amount of money to show and a certain amount of money to win each fight of the three fights. I was supposed to fight Bas Rutten in UFC Brazil. They came back and said, 'Well, we're not going to pay you what the contract says.' They offered me a little over a quarter what the contract said they were supposed to pay me and basically said take it or leave it. I said, 'I'm prepared to fight, I want to fight, but if you're not going to honor the contract, I'm not going to fight.'"

Couture ended up walking out of UFC as the UFC Heavyweight champion, never having defended the title. UFC promptly stripped him of the belt and moved on to other business.

He disappeared from the MMA scene for nearly a year before returning to take on Enson Inoue at Vale Tudo Japan '98 on October 25, 1998. Couture went into the fight undefeated in MMA competition, but he didn't leave as such. Inoue, considered a very tough fighter (albeit not the most skilled), was nevertheless able to submit Couture with an armbar just under two minutes into their match.

After such a long absence, Couture's return to the sport was a disappointment, and his next fight certainly didn't improve his situation either. On March 20, 1999, Couture made his debut with the RINGS promotion, taking on Russian fighter Mikhail Illoukhine.

Illoukhine, like Inoue, was a fighter considered both very good and very tough, but not one of the very best MMA had to offer. Couture and Illoukhine battled for over seven minutes, to a fluke ending: Couture and Illoukhine were being repositioned in the ring after a break, and Illoukhine armbarred Couture. One might think that this result should have been vetoed by RINGS, but it stood. Couture hadn't won a fight since walking out of UFC.

On October 9, 2000, Couture entered the first round of the annual RINGS King of Kings tournament at Yoyogi National Stadium Gym II in Tokyo. Couture's first opponent of the night was the formidable, but smaller, Jeremy Horn. Couture managed to defeat Horn by unanimous decision. He followed up this win by defeating Pancrase veteran Ryushi Yanagisawa via majority decision later in the night to advance to the third round of the tournament, on February 24, 2001.

Although Couture had finally found success outside UFC with his wins over Horn and Yanagisawa in RINGS, most still believed he was only a mediocre fighter who held a chance victory over Belfort and a dull victory over Maurice Smith, who was primarily a kickboxer. Couture just wasn't considered a top-level talent.

Couture proved this to be complete hogwash when he and SEG settled their differences, and "The Natural" returned to the octagon for the first time in many years. There he took on the reigning UFC Heavyweight champion: Kevin "The Monster" Randleman.

Randleman, who had trained under Mark Coleman, had freakish athletic ability and amazing wrestling skills that sent him to the top of the UFC's Heavyweight division. His rise came at a time when the promotion was at a very low level of popularity, however, so in general, MMA competition in North America wasn't particularly strong. Couture's opportunity here was to come back and win the title that he had never lost inside the octagon. Most people saw him as the aged former champion coming back to inevitably lose to the current, highly skilled champion in a passing-of-the-torch deal.

Couture would again be going into a major fight as the underdog.

In this fight, Couture again proved the dominance of Greco-Roman wrestling as a mixed martial arts skill, just as he had against Vitor Belfort years earlier. He was able to tie Randleman up in a clinch and tire him out, and although Randleman, a very skilled wrestler, initially appeared to be the superior athlete, Couture took him down in the end, pounding him until the ref stopped the fight.

With this win, not only did Couture win back a title that he'd never actually lost, but he also set a record, becoming the first two-time UFC champion in company history. The fight against Randleman was a big turning point in the UFC's existence, as Larry Hazzard of the New Jersey Athletic Control Board watched the match and, noting the display of sportsmanship before and after the contest by Couture and Randleman, decided to approve UFC to run in the state of New Jersey. The Nevada State Athletic Commission followed suit. This relieved most of the political pressure on UFC, and the promotion returned to cable in late 2001, shortly after Zuffa purchased the company.

On February 24, 2001, a few months after the Randleman fight, Couture returned to Japan to compete in the final event of RINGS's King of Kings tournament. His first opponent of the evening was Tsuyoshi Kohsaka, a top Japanese fighter and longtime RINGS competitor who had fought in UFC and trained with Frank Shamrock and Maurice Smith. Couture defeated Kohsaka via unanimous decision, and this sent him to the semifinals of the large tournament.

Couture's next opponent was future PRIDE veteran Valentijn Overeem. Somewhat shockingly, Overeem submitted Couture with a guillotine choke in only fifty-six seconds, showing that Couture, who still wore the UFC Heavyweight title, had yet to become completely adept with submissions defense. RINGS also favored standup fighting as it was illegal to punch your opponent in the head on the ground, and referees stood the fighters up much quicker in this organization than in UFC. The Japanese branch of RINGS actually ended up folding not long after this tournament was held.

After the loss to Overeem in the semifinals of the King of Kings tournament, his last fight outside of UFC, Couture returned to UFC to take part in one of the most vicious fights ever put on inside the octagon. He went up against highly skilled striker and top UFC heavyweight contender Pedro Rizzo.

The fight against Rizzo, the first of Couture's two encounters with him in UFC, took place on May 4, 2001. It was an absolute war. Again, Couture went into the fight as the major underdog, and again, he came out the victor—but only by the slimmest of margins.

"Pedro Rizzo the first time was definitely the toughest fight I have been in to date," says Couture in an interview with Matt Shickell for SFUK. "Even with the Ricco [Rodriguez] fight getting hurt, and the Belfort fight getting hurt, that is the toughest fight . . . five rounds of just brawling . . . that I have ever been in."

Couture dominated the first round of the fight by taking Rizzo down and making him bleed, and pounded Rizzo so badly, just seconds before the end of the round, that the fight could easily have been stopped. But it wasn't, and it continued into round two looking like Couture would have the upper hand.

But that wasn't the case, as Rizzo turned the tables, murdering Couture throughout the second round, and making him bleed. The fight could have been stopped in round two in favor of Rizzo, but Couture, although damaged, survived into the next round, and this enabled him to even things out some. The fight continued through the fourth and fifth rounds, even though both fighters were clearly exhausted and in pain, and it ended up going to the time limit.

Watching the fight, you wouldn't have had any idea who won on the judges' scorecards, because it was a vicious battle in which both competitors gave and took tons of damage. No matter who won the decision, it would be controversial. Of course, Couture, on pure guts and bravery, ended up winning the decision; the surprising part was that it was a unanimous decision. But with a fight this close, there was bound to be a rematch.

And there was a rematch, on November 2, 2001, at UFC 34. It was a very different fight from the first time Rizzo and Couture had met a few months earlier, except that, despite having taken home the decision in the first fight, Couture was still considered the major underdog against Rizzo.

Couture trained with his former foe Maurice Smith for the fight in standup, and came into his rematch with Rizzo prepared. He shocked everyone by manhandling Rizzo, who cuts easily, making him bleed and taking him down to pound him on the ground. Couture punished Rizzo until the fight was stopped early in the third round. With the win, Couture managed to retain his UFC Heavyweight title, proving that, in the end, he was the better competitor and deserved to be champion, no matter how close his first fight with Rizzo had been.

The next challenger to Couture's Heavyweight title was Josh Barnett, a charismatic fighter who had been moving up the UFC heavyweight ranks quickly with wins over Gan McGee, Semmy Schilt, and Bobby Hoffman. In fact, Barnett's only career loss up until that point had been against Rizzo, via knockout.

Barnett versus Couture took place on March 22, 2002, at UFC 36 in Las Vegas. Couture had earned new respect as champion after destroying Pedro Rizzo in their rematch late in 2001, and many favored Couture going into the fight against Barnett, confident that Couture would walk out of the octagon still the UFC Heavyweight champion.

But that was not the case. Barnett, an excellent and very well-rounded fighter, had a considerable size and strength advantage over Couture (a "small" heavyweight), and although Couture used his dynamic wrestling skill to keep Barnett at bay early in the fight, Barnett used his size advantage exceedingly well during the latter part of the bout. Barnett used his size so well, in fact, that Couture gassed out in the second round, and Barnett was able to pound him for the stoppage at 4:35 of that round in an exciting fight.

Not only had Couture lost the UFC Heavyweight title, but also, for the first time in his career, he had lost a fight inside the octagon. Couture, known for being one of the truly greatest sportsmen in MMA, showed his gentle-manly nature by putting the title on Barnett after the match.

It seemed that Couture was out of the Heavyweight title picture, but as it turned out, this wasn't to be the case at all. A strange situation arose when Barnett, despite his "pudgy" appearance (proving that not only muscle-bound bodybuilder types use steroids), tested positive for anabolic steroids after the fight, and was subsequently suspended from fighting in Nevada by the Nevada State Athletic Commission. He was stripped of the UFC Heavy-weight title without ever once having defended it.

UFC decided to put the title up for grabs between the former champion Couture and top contender Ricco Rodriguez at UFC 39 on September 27, 2002. Couture would get a chance to recapture the Heavyweight title and redeem himself, albeit against a different opponent than the one he had lost the belt to.

Much like the Barnett fight, Couture went into this bout as the heavy favorite, since many people didn't see Rodriguez as being on the same level as him. But much like Barnett had, Rodriguez used his considerable size ad-vantage to damage Couture. Although Couture's wrestling skill helped him to win the early rounds of the fight, he eventually gassed out, and Rodriguez' size was too much. In the fifth and final round of the fight, Rodriguez had Cou-ture on the ground, pounding him badly enough that Couture tapped out at 3:04 of the fight, and the vacant UFC Heavyweight title went to Rodriguez.

"I think if anything, in the Ricco fight I was overprepared. I trained too hard. And consequently wore down in the later rounds," Couture tells Schickell. "I learned a valuable lesson, and it's been kind of an ongoing process of finding that fine line between overdoing it and doing enough, and peaking at the right time is a big part of the equation." Couture suffered a broken orbital bone because of the fight, and ended up on the shelf for a few months.

Closing in on the age of forty, Couture had lost his last two fights in a manner that convinced many that his days as a top-level fighter were over. Because of the losses, his age, and his injured orbital bone, many felt that he should retire from MMA.

Couture was actually going to continue to compete in the Heavyweight division, but a strange situation arose, changing both Couture and UFC in ways that no one would have expected.

Tito Ortiz, at that time the UFC's dominating Light-Heavyweight champion and arguably their biggest star, had a contract impasse with the company, and it looked like he wouldn't be returning to UFC anytime soon. Many people felt that Ortiz was ducking the number-one contender to his championship title, Chuck Liddell, who had handled Tito in training sessions years earlier. Whatever the reason was for Tito's absence, UFC decided to schedule Liddell in a fight at UFC 43 on June 6, 2003, for an interim version of the Light-Heavyweight title, the idea being that once Tito came back—if he ever came back—the interim Light-Heavyweight champion would fight him to unify the two versions of the title. UFC planned to replace Ortiz with Liddell as the company's main-event star, and all they needed was someone who wouldn't have much of a chance against Liddell to go in there for an impressive loss.

Enter Randy Couture. Most felt the aged Heavyweight champion would be a tomato can if fed to Liddell, the company's new big star. Couture had never fought in Light-Heavyweight before, and had to cut weight to make that division. Since Ken Shamrock had lost badly when he fought Tito Ortiz in November 2002 after cutting weight from Heavyweight to Light-Heavyweight, it looked like something similar might happen to Couture when he stepped in against Liddell.

"I had friends [who said], 'You need to go down to Light-Heavyweight. These guys are too big. You used to wrestle at 198. You should be fighting at 205. Somebody needs to shut Tito up. Why don't you go down and do it?'" Couture tells Schickell, "and all that kind of stuff from my friends. And after the Ricco fight it made a lot of sense. The guys were just getting too big in the Heavyweight division. And they're not just big guys like the first guys I fought. They know how to fight, and weight becomes a huge advantage [to them]."

UFC believed that since Liddell was very good at avoiding takedowns, Couture wouldn't be able to take him down. Liddell would pick Couture apart standing, and because of Couture's age, he would eventually gas out, and that would be all she wrote.

Well, everyone was in for a shocker. Again, Couture trained with his former opponent Maurice Smith in standup, and he used his skills at dirty boxing from within the clinch to actually beat Liddell on his feet. Couture picked Liddell apart for the entire fight, until the referee stepped in at 2:39 of the third round. It was one of the biggest upsets in UFC history: Couture had cut down a weight division, and came back from a bad injury and two bad losses to outstrike and defeat Chuck Liddell, one of the best strikers in the world, to win the interim Light-Heavyweight title. Once again, Randy Couture had overcome seemingly insurmountable odds.

In winning the interim Light-Heavyweight championship, Couture became the first fighter in UFC to win titles at two different weight levels. He is what most people consider to be the most accomplished mixed martial artist of all time.

"Randy had no marketing, and no one gave a crap about him, and despite that, in the last couple of years when he was supposed to be over the hill, he's annihilated his opponents," says Jeff Osborne in an interview conducted for this book. "He's an analyzer, and he watches tapes of fights. He's forty and doing things in better shape than half the fighters younger than him will ever accomplish."

Couture's next opponent was to be Vitor Belfort, who had made quick work of Marvin Eastman at UFC 43 in a rematch of their UFC 15 fight. But suddenly, Tito Ortiz was back in the picture, and he wanted to unify the two versions of the Light-Heavyweight title. Belfort had to wait, as Couture versus Ortiz was booked for UFC 44 at Mandalay Bay in Las Vegas on September 26, 2003. Tito was younger, considered to be in his prime, hadn't lost a fight in years, and had never been put on his back in MMA. Many people, including Tito himself, were confident that Couture would be out-wrestled in Vegas that day.

Couture, again going in with the odds stacked against him, showed everyone why he is Randy Couture by putting Tito on his back in the first round alone. Tito wasn't able to put Couture on his back even once throughout the entire fight, although he tried hard to do so.

After every round, it was expected that Couture would tire out, and the more-powerful Ortiz would take control and pound him. But Couture kept going out there fresh as a daisy, and he kept putting Ortiz down on his back on the canvas. In the fourth round, Couture even got full mount and pounded Ortiz to a near stoppage, although Ortiz survived to make it to the fifth. In the closing seconds of the final round, Couture actually managed to take Ortiz down with a suplex and, to really highlight what he'd done to Ortiz in this fight, with seconds ticking off the clock, Couture stood over Ortiz, and spanked him. Ortiz had been systematically dismantled by a better wrestler, and Couture was now the undisputed UFC Light-Heavyweight champion.

"I said all along that anything he did, I could do just that little bit better, and it was going to come down to wrestling," says Couture when interviewed for this book. "I watched all of his matches, ninety-nine percent of them he won by taking the guy down and getting on top. And I was sure that there was no way, without a real struggle, he was going to take me down. And it came down to who got that top position."

Couture, at forty, had rebounded from two losses at the Heavyweight level over the UFC Heavyweight title to two wins at the Light-Heavyweight level over the UFC Light-Heavyweight title. Now the undisputed champion, Couture's roller-coaster ride wouldn't stop, as he would have to continue to defend the championship title. And his first defense would be against Vitor Belfort.

The rematch of their UFC 15 bout, at UFC 46 on January 31, 2004, was marred by strange circumstances. Having defeated Belfort the first time, Couture was the favorite going into the match, but the fight almost never happened because Belfort's sister, who lived in Brazil, disappeared just days before the fight was to take place. Surprisingly, despite his family concerns and the amount of stress he was under, Belfort didn't pull out of the match.

No one knew how the situation would affect Belfort when it came to the fight with Couture. In the end, no one would ever find out, either. Just seconds after the fight began, Belfort threw a punch, and his glove grazed Randy Couture's eye, badly cutting him. Couture started to wince in pain, the fight was stopped, and the ringside doctor stepped in to check out his eye, ending the fight. Despite barely doing anything in the fight and having been in the octagon for less than a minute, Belfort was the new Light-Heavyweight champion because the fight was stopped due to an injury from a completely legal punch. Belfort had not poked Couture in the eye, but his glove cut Couture. When a fight is stopped due to a cut, the title changes hands. It was a strange way to cut short what could have been an exciting match.

And when the rematch took place, on August 21, 2004, at UFC 49, it was an exciting match—or rather another exciting win for Randy Couture—and Couture became the first two-time Light-Heavyweight champion in UFC history when he was able to take Belfort down and pound him for the majority of the fight. It ended after the third round when Belfort had taken enough punishment and was bleeding profusely due to a huge gash on his head.

Whether Couture, now in his early forties, will be able to hold off Father Time just once more (until the next fight, of course), and come out on top again, or if his age will finally catch up with him to begin the downward spiral of one of the most legendary careers in MMA history has yet to be seen. Maybe their rematch will be like a Rocky movie, where the champ takes a freaky loss at the beginning, but returns at the end to vanquish his enemy. Randy Couture can't last forever. Even Rocky Balboa got old and retired. But, as UFC's greatest underdog, he's lasted much longer than most would have thought possible.

Don Frye

With his Tom Selleck–look-alike mustache and face, chiseled musculature, and a charismatic persona like something out of a violent spaghetti western, Don "The Predator" Frye, one of the biggest stars the UFC produced during its glory period and one of the biggest all-time foreign names in Japan, is the very definition of the term "tough guy," who brought his now-legendary never-say-die attitude to mixed martial arts.

Frye was born on November 23, 1965. His family was always moving around, as his father was a lieutenant colonel in the U.S. Air Force. "About the time I wore out my welcome in the town, it was time to leave," jokes Frye in an interview that was conducted for this book. After relocating to many different states many different times, Frye's family settled in Arizona when he was about fourteen.

He started to wrestle in high school, eventually for his high school's varsity team. After high school, Frye went on to wrestle for Arizona State University, where Dan Severn was an assistant coach. It was this connection that would later lead Frye into the UFC.

In 1988, Frye suffered a season-ending shoulder injury, and was out of action when Arizona State won the national title that year. Frye recovered from the injury, and successfully competed for Arizona State until he was recruited by Oklahoma State and competed for a season there.

Before he made his way into the UFC in 1996, Frye participated in judo, earning a second-degree black belt, and also boxed professionally, composing a respectable 5-2-1 record in that sport. Evidence of his tough-guy attitude and his absolute will to both fight and win, Frye took part in his first professional boxing match after just three months of training. "I was supposed to train for a year, and then they would turn me pro, but after about four or five months they thought I was ready, so they turned me pro," he recalls.

After eight pro boxing bouts, Frye decided that boxing wasn't for him, and he hung the gloves up. "The thing is, I was good, but not great," said Frye in an interview for Erich Krauss's *Brawl*. "And only great guys make it. But I was good enough to get out at the right time."

Frye went on to work as a firefighter for a number of years, and dealt with a failed marriage. "I was in a bad marriage and it killed the athlete in me," says Frye in an interview with Sherdog.com. "I had gotten married and was just going along with my life as it was. That was my mistake. So when I got divorced it sort of opened me back up. A divorce either makes or breaks you. I think it was one of the best things that ever happened to me."

At this point, Frye saw Dan Severn win the UFC 5 tournament by defeating Dave Beneteau in the finals, and he decided to give Severn a call to see if he could get into the UFC. "Dan was coming to Arizona to train, and he needed a training partner, so I was basically his main throwing dummy for the Ultimate Ultimate '95," Frye recalls in Krass's *Brawl*. "He ended up winning, and he put in a good word for me with the UFC."

Frye began to train with Severn for his UFC debut at UFC 8 on February 16, 1996. The event was held in Puerto Rico due to political heat back in the United States. In addition to training with Severn, Frye also competed in an underground no-holds-barred event in Atlanta, where he took on an ex-navy SEAL and submitted him with a choke.

Frye was in the first round of the UFC 8 tournament, taking on street fighter Thomas Ramirez. The event was dubbed "David versus Goliath" due to its theme of pitting huge fighters against smaller opponents. Frye knocked Ramirez out in eight seconds flat, making the fight one of the quickest in UFC history. "When I first started out I was a fireman and on my days off I was shoeing horses out here in Arizona," says Frye in *Brawl* about his early involvement in UFC. "I was working six to seven days a week, plus training."

The win propelled Frye into the second round, where he took on Sam Adkins, and again made quick work of his opponent by taking him down and stopping him with strikes. This win sent Frye into the tournament finals.

Frye's final opponent of the night was Canadian powerhouse Gary Goodridge, who outweighed Frye by at least twenty-five pounds and was also making his UFC debut at this event. Goodridge was able to throw Frye around early on in the bout, but despite his massive size advantage, Frye was able to defeat the bigger man just over two minutes into the match.

The charismatic and highly skilled Frye had quickly proven himself by winning his debut UFC tournament, and UFC had a new star on their hands. Showing the extent of Frye's star power with UFC at that time, he was featured in an article in *People Magazine* shortly after the UFC 8 tournament win.

Frye, who by this point had started using the nickname of "The Predator" as a play off of Dan Severn's nickname of "The Beast," returned to prove himself in a singles bout against a top jiu jitsu player, Carlson Gracie trainee Amaury Bitetti, at UFC 9 in Detroit, as there was no tournament scheduled for that event.

Ever since Royce Gracie had left the UFC some time earlier, UFC had been looking for a new highly skilled Brazilian Jiu Jitsu fighter to take Royce's place at the top of the promotion. There was a possibility that Bitetti, who replaced legendary vale tudo fighter Marco Ruas in the UFC 9 fight against Frye, could have been that fighter.

Frye put a quick stop to any success Bitetti might have had in UFC by handing him one of the meanest beatings in the promotion's history. Frye had a significant weight advantage on Bitetti, and used it well, as Bitetti was never able to take Frye down during their fight.

Frye pounded Bitetti with punches and knees standing up, and when they wound up on the ground, he delivered more devastating knees to Bitetti's head, bruising and bloodying the Brazilian fighter badly enough that, with just a couple of minutes left on the clock, referee John McCarthy stepped in and stopped the bout.

Frye was back at UFC 10 on July 12, 1996, to compete in two of the toughest bouts of his life. He suffered his first loss in MMA and his only loss in the sport until November 2002 in PRIDE. Despite the fact that he inevitably lost in the tournament finals, it was ironically Frye's losing performance in the tournament that cemented his reputation as a very tough fighter who would never say quit.

UFC returned to the tournament format for this show. Frye's first bout of the night was against Mark Hall in the quarterfinals. Frye took Hall down early in the fight and pounded on him on the ground, but it took him over ten minutes to ice Hall off, as Hall wouldn't give in to Frye's barrage of strikes. Although Frye easily dominated the bout, it took a lot of gas out of him before the second round of the tournament, where he met one of the toughest foes of his career: Brian Johnston.

Although, a couple of years down the line, Frye and Johnston became friends and worked together in New Japan Pro Wrestling, they were anything but friends as they stepped into the octagon that night. Johnston used his kickboxing abilities to wear out the already-tired Frye, until Johnston himself gassed and Frye took him to the ground, slaughtering him with elbows and opening up a cut on Johnston's forehead. Johnston tapped out at 4:37 of the fight. "The Brian Johnston fight, that was the only time I thought about quitting," said Frye in an interview with Sherdog.com in 2000. "He hit me a couple of times, gave me a knee, it went through my mind!"

Having fought, and won, two very hard fights against opponents he'd underestimated, Frye was worn down. And things were about to get worse; Frye's opponent for the final match would be Mark Coleman, an excellent and very powerful wrestler with a thirty-pound weight advantage over Frye who had debuted in UFC that night and made it to the finals by defeating Moti Horenstein in the first round and Frye's opponent from the finals of the UFC 8 tournament, Gary Goodridge, in the second round.

The fight would be Frye's first, last, and only loss in UFC, and his only loss in MMA for years. Although Frye lost the fight, the beating that he took and the fact that he never gave in solidified his reputation with mixed martial arts fans across the globe.

At the time, Coleman was managed by Frye's ex-manager, Richard Hamilton, who held a personal grudge against Frye. Coleman destroyed Frye with an onslaught of hard strikes, closing both of Frye's eyes and making hamburger meat out of Frye's face. The overhead shot of both fighters standing as Coleman batters Frye against the fence is a legendary video clip in MMA, and proof of the beating that Frye took that night. John McCarthy stopped the fight once to check Frye's cuts, and he stepped in again at just over eleven minutes into the punishment to end the bout and give Coleman the tournament win. Frye never gave in. He spent the night in the hospital. In fact, Frye has never tapped out in his entire career. He is one of a very small handful of fighters at this level in MMA who can claim that.

Frye returned to MMA a few months later at U-Japan, an event featuring a variety of UFC fighters put on by Robert DePersia, Frye's agent at the time, in Japan on November 17, 1996. Frye took on Mark Hall, his opponent from the first round of the UFC 9 tournament who was also managed by DePersia, and submitted him with a forearm choke at 5:29 of the bout.

Back in the UFC a month later, DePersia's role as agent for both Frye and Hall led to an interesting situation. In December 1995, UFC put on its first of two Ultimate Ultimate tournaments. It featured many of the biggest-name fighters within the organization, and was won by Dan Severn. On December 7, 1996, the second of the two Ultimate Ultimates took place. This tournament, considered the most loaded in MMA history up to that point in time, retained this status until PRIDE held its first Grand Prix tournament in 2000.

The tournament featured Frye, Brian Johnston, Ken Shamrock, Tank Abbott, Gary Goodridge, Cal Worsham, Kimo Leopoldo, and Paul Varelans. Nearly every fighter in it would end up doing worked pro wrestling at some point down the road. Frye's first-round opponent was Gary Goodridge, who had given Frye hell in the finals of the UFC 8 tournament.

Goodridge wore Frye out once again, using his size and strength advantage until Goodridge gassed out and submitted at 11:19 due to exhaustion. Following this first-round fight against Goodridge, and reminiscent of the UFC 10 tournament, Frye fought a punishing uphill battle against fatigue to make it to the finals.

But something strange happened in the second round. Kimo Leopoldo would have been Frye's opponent had he defeated the giant Paul Varelans in the first round of the tournament, but he pulled out, putting Frye's two-time opponent Mark Hall in Kimo's spot as an alternate. Hall had earned the alternate's spot by quickly defeating Felix Lee Mitchell earlier in the evening.

Frye had already defeated Hall twice. Only those involved will ever know the full, true story, but Hall claims that, since both he and Frye were managed by Robert DePersia at the time, he was approached backstage before the fight by both Frye and DePersia. They wanted him to throw the fight. The reasoning they gave was that Frye had already defeated Hall twice, that Hall was not on his level, and that Frye had expended a lot of energy fighting Gary Goodridge in the first round and needed all the energy he could muster for the finals. Hall claims they offered him some of Frye's purse if Frye won the tournament in exchange for doing the job.

The fight looked fishy, as Frye took Hall down and submitted him with a heel hook in less than a minute. Frye is definitely not considered a top-tier submissions expert, and he never used leg locks to win a fight either before or after this bout.

"I had no involvement, whether that's true or not [that Hall took a dive]. If something like that happened, he decided he didn't want to get his ass whooped, and he made a deal with somebody else," says Frye, when interviewed for this book, regarding the possibility of this bout against Hall being worked. "I was just as perplexed as everyone else, probably more so."

Nevertheless, although the controversy stemming from the bout put a damper on Frye's eventual tournament win, the match did send Frye into the finals.

His opponent was the colorful Tank Abbott, who had made quick work of both Cal Worsham and alternate Steve Nelmark in the first and second rounds of the tournament to make it into the finals. Never known for being a highly skilled fighter, Tank had gained a reputation as a brawler with heavy hands and would be looking to go toe-to-toe with Frye in the tournament finals.

Frye was looking for the same thing. He made the near-fatal error of deciding to wage a standup war against Tank Abbott. Abbott rocked Frye with hard punches in the opening seconds of the fight, and although Frye had boxed professionally in the past and Tank was merely a tough brawler, Tank out-duelled Frye on their feet. Fortunately for Frye, he accidentally stepped on Tank's foot, causing the massive Abbott to crash to the canvas, where Frye hooked him in a rear naked choke to submit Tank at only 1:22 of the bout. If the accidental tripping hadn't occurred, it may have been a different story for Frye, although that's pure speculation, as Tank, unlike Frye, has never been known for going the distance in a war. There's a strong likelihood that Frye would have been able to secure the victory down the line nevertheless. "I really don't have a game plan. I'm not smart enough for a game plan," jokes Frye in an interview for Sherdog.com. "The thing is, I like to look the critter in the eye. I have a stupid streak. . . . I like to beat the guys at their own game. That's why I fought Abbott standing up; that's why I fought Bitetti on the ground. Just to see if I could do it."

"I broke my hand [fighting Tank] and had to get two pins put in it," adds Frye. "Then when the next UFC came I wanted to fight. I wanted to fight Severn for the [Superfight title]. But I guess the UFC had other plans, as it did not happen."

Frye won the 1996 Ultimate Ultimate tournament—arguably the biggest tournament UFC had ever put on—securing himself as a top fighter in UFC and silencing any doubts following his loss to Mark Coleman in the finals of UFC 10. It would be his final appearance in the UFC.

Frye was one of the UFC's biggest stars at the time, having first won the UFC 8 tournament and then of course the '96 Ultimate Ultimate after he placed in the finals of the UFC 10 tournament. He was never positioned in a Superfight main event in his UFC run, though, as his only non-tournament fight in UFC was against Amaury Bitetti in the undercard of UFC 9. He would have been the biggest star on the UFC 10 card, a card that drew a very disappointing buyrate of 0.43 on pay-per-view, the lowest buyrate UFC had done since their very first event in November 1993. UFC 10 came directly after the very dull Shamrock-Severn fight at UFC 9, however, and that fight damaged UFC's business enough that UFC 10 was going to draw a lower buyrate no matter what, so the low buyrate can't be attributed to any lack of box-office drawing power on Frye's part. Also, the '96 Ultimate Ultimate only drew a 0.5 buyrate, half of what the first version of the tournament did a year earlier, but this was due to the overall declining popularity of the product rather than the lack of drawing power of any one fighter in the tournament.

Frye was the first athlete in UFC history to have a background of competing in amateur wrestling at a high level and a background of boxing professionally, and this helped to make him one of the most influential fighters in MMA history. Prior to Frye, each fighter in the UFC was seen as representing one individual fighting style. Frye was the first fighter to be considered a "master" of two different styles (boxing and wrestling), and this set the tone for fighters down the line, like Frank Shamrock and Tito Ortiz in the late '90s and everyone else since, who cross-train in every fighting style that could be of use in MMA.

"Where wrestler Dan Severn was not the best striker, Don Frye, another man with a wrestling background, was that guy that people had been worrying would eventually show up on the scene: the wrestler who could box," says Stephen Quadros. "Although he wasn't a top-level wrestler or boxer separately, when he put the two skills together in MMA it was frightening."

Following the '96 Ultimate Ultimate, UFC 12, in February 1997, was the UFC's final show available on cable. The cable ban forced the UFC to air their pay-per-views on the satellite systems and on the odd cable system, and this lowered their fan base to just a fraction of what it once was. UFC didn't have the money to pay some of their bigger-name fighters, and throughout 1997 and into '98, many fighters left the promotion.

Frye was among those fighters who left UFC for a better money offer from New Japan Pro Wrestling. "They were looking for a UFC fighter. Originally they wanted Ken Shamrock, for obvious reasons—because of all the titles that he won," recalls Frye in *Brawl*. "He negotiated a deal, and they gave him a contract. Then he ran over to the WWF. So they were out a UFC fighter. Brad Rheingans, who was the American booker for New Japan, was friends with Jeff Blatnick. He called Jeff and asked whom he would recommend. Jeff, being a great guy, recommended me."

Frye had a very successful career with New Japan, making his debut in August of 1997 and becoming the foreign attraction for pro wrestling in Japan until the emergence of Bob Sapp. He was a foreign heel in New Japan, feuding with the native heroes. One of the only wrestlers to have defeated native superstar Naoya Ogawa twice in pro wrestling, Frye defeated Ogawa at the January 4, 1998, Tokyo Dome show in front of 65,000 fans, and gained another victory over him at the Tokyo Dome on April 4, 1998, in front of 70,000 fans. This led to Frye being the opponent for Japanese icon Antonio Inoki's retirement match at the end of the night, which Frye lost. Frye, who had come into the company with fellow former UFC fighters Brian Johnston and Dave Beneteau to form the heel group Club 245 (245 being the penal code in California for "assault with intent to do major bodily harm"), also challenged for the company's most-coveted title, the IWGP Heavyweight championship, but was defeated by then-champion Keiji Mutoh in April 1999, again at the Tokyo Dome.

The move to New Japan elevated Frye's name value with the Japanese audience, and his success in New Japan was a major precursor for other mixed martial artists to enter into pro wrestling in Japan. After spending a number of years wrestling for New Japan, the opportunity arose for Frye to return to the world of MMA competition when PRIDE offered him a contract in 2001.

His first fight back would be on September 24, 2001, at PRIDE 16, where he took on Gilbert Yvel, a Dutch kickboxer who didn't have much experience fighting on the ground, but who was known for his mean streak. Yvel was also very good standing, and Frye's reputation as a tough-guy pro wrestler would take a major hit in Japan if he was defeated badly on his feet by Yvel. It was a major risk for Frye, because a bad loss would permanently damage his reputation, especially after so many years away from actual competition.

Frye, who went into the fight just two weeks after tearing his quad, was able to take Yvel down and pound him during the fight, but overall he was on the losing end of the battle. Yvel was disqualified at 7:27 of the first round, however, for holding onto the ropes to avoid a takedown at three different points, and this gave Frye the win.

Frye's next fight would be against another fighter primarily known as a kickboxer, Cyril Abidi, who had never competed in an MMA-rules bout in his career up to that point in time, although he had been training for a few weeks with Frank Shamrock leading up to the fight. Frye's fight with Abidi took place on New Year's Eve, 2001, at that year's version of Antonio Inoki's Bom Ba Ye event in Japan, which had a theme of K-1 kickboxers (like Abidi) against New Japan pro wrestlers (like Frye).

Abidi's experience in fighting on the ground was limited, and he was submitted by Frye at 0:21 of the second round of an exciting bout. Frye had won the first two fights of his MMA comeback, and he would go on to win two in a row after this, as well.

Shamrock versus Frye finally took place on February 24, 2002, at PRIDE 19. Wrestling fans on both sides of the Pacific were geared up for the fight.

The bout went down as an all-time classic fight in mixed martial arts. Although the second round of the fight was slow, both fighters exploded in the third round, in which Frye knocked Shamrock down.

It was a very close fight. Shamrock had made numerous attempts at leglocks and heel hooks in the fight, and Frye's refusal to give up in any submission hold would cost him dearly later on, as the leglocks Shamrock caught him in ripped up Frye's knees and ankles badly. Whoever lost the bout would most likely be seen as the more overrated of the two legendary fighters by mixed martial arts fans, so it was a very important bout. The fight was also a big deal because it was the last fight on Shamrock's huge contract with PRIDE. Whoever lost the bout may not have been in for a contract renewal, and whoever won would be looking at bigger-money fights down the line with PRIDE. Frye ended up winning a split-decision, exchanging his long-term physical health for long-term payoffs from PRIDE. Shamrock's contract was not renewed. "I thought it was my best fight, and I thought it was Ken's best fight too," says Frye in an interview conducted for this book.

The fight was a fairly big hit in the U.S., where it aired on same-day tape delay, doing a buyrate on North American pay-per-view that was significantly higher than any PRIDE pay-per-view prior to it. PRIDE officials figured that this bout would break PRIDE in as a major promotion in the United States, but this didn't happen because neither Frye's nor Shamrock's respective name values were able to get them covered by any mainstream U.S. media.

Frye followed this classic MMA war with yet another war-like fight that went down as one of the most exciting bouts in MMA history when he took on the very popular pro wrestler Yoshihiro Takayama on June 23, 2002, at PRIDE 21 at Super Saitama Arena.

Takayama was famous in Japan for being a superstar pro wrestler, but he had never won a legit mixed martial arts bout. In Japan, however, it's about the journey and not the destination, and Takayama went out of his way to have very exciting fights, often at his own great physical expense. Takayama would always come out of his fights hurting badly. In that way, he's much like Don Frye, so all signs indicated that this would be a violent battle before it even happened.

Originally, Frye's opponent for the fight was to be Mark Coleman. Frye had wanted to get Coleman back into the ring since losing to him in the UFC 10 tournament finals many years earlier. They wouldn't meet again yet, though, as Coleman suffered an injury before the fight could go down, so Takayama was brought in as a high-profile replacement.

Frye punished Takayama for over six minutes until the referee stopped the fight. It was one of the most brutal MMA fights in history, as both men went out there and threw caution and sanity to the wind, pulverizing each other. "There were several punches that made me see stars," said Frye in a post-fight interview with PRIDE. "I got kneed, and I bet my ribs are turning blue. My teeth really hurt too."

Although Takayama is not a truly skilled fighter, he is very exciting when he fights. Frye is a pure fighter at heart, and this gave him the win. "Takayama is really a tough fighter," Frye continues . "I think he's the toughest fighter I've fought up until now. It was a great fight."

The bout is seen as one of the greatest in PRIDE history, because it was the definition of what people want MMA to be: a fight where both competitors go out to the ring for an exciting and brutal standup war.

Whether or not having two of the most exciting and brutal matches in MMA history back-to-back is worth the amount of pain and injuries sustained by the fighters is up for debate.

Frye's next bout was fought under K-1 kickboxing rules at PRIDE's huge co-promotional show with K-1 at the then–National Stadium in Kokuritsu, Japan, on August 28, 2002, in front of 71,000 fans paying $7 million U.S. This set the all-time record for highest gate to a pro wrestling/mixed martial arts event. Replacing the injured K-1 star Mark Hunt, Frye took on top-tier K-1 superstar Jerome LeBanner, who would go in to make the finals of the K-1 Grand Prix later that year.

Not many people gave Frye a chance in this fight because of his lack of experience under K-1 rules and the fact that LeBanner was one of that promotion's top kickboxers. LeBanner knocked Frye out less than two minutes into the fight.

When asked in a post-fight interview with PRIDE about was going through his mind during the fight with LeBanner, Frye simply responded, "Leather." When asked what went through his mind directly after the fight, Frye elaborated by saying, "The taste of leather."

The loss, much like Ken Shamrock's kickboxing loss in Pancrase or Royce Gracie's loss to Wallid Ismael in jiu jitsu, wasn't very damaging to Frye's reputation as a tough guy and top-tier fighter in MMA because people recognized that K-1, a standup fighting sport, is very different from MMA, and is something Frye did not have a lot of experience in. As far as MMA fans were concerned, Frye had not lost an MMA-rules bout since his loss to Coleman at UFC 10 many years earlier, he had won his four MMA fights since his return to competition in 2001, and he remained undefeated in PRIDE.

Well, that was about to change. Hidehiko Yoshida had debuted with PRIDE on the August 2002 stadium show that saw Frye lose to LeBanner under K-1 rules. Yoshida, a national sports hero in Japan, was a master judoka, capturing gold at the 172-pound level in that sport at the '92 Olympics in Barcelona. His gold-medal victory was considered an amazing performance of that era. Yoshida was just out of his prime in judoka when he entered MMA, though, as he had been a world champion in judo in 1999 and a gold medal favorite at the 2000 Olympics until he broke his arm and was not able to continue his second quest for Olympic gold. At the National Stadium show in August 2002, Yoshida had defeated the legendary Royce Gracie in controversial fashion, as Yoshida seemed very close to finishing Royce off in their bout when the referee stopped the fight and awarded the win to Yoshida. The problem was that, under the rules of that fight, the referee was not allowed to stop the bout, but he did so anyways.

The Japanese audience saw Yoshida as one of the greatest submission experts of this era and an all-time great judoka. However, the consensus among North American MMA fans was that Yoshida was a fraud because his win over Royce was phony, since the referee had stopped that bout, giving the win to Yoshida, when the rules stated for that fight that it couldn't be stopped by the referee. North American MMA fans thought he was a cheat and screwed Royce Gracie out of a victory in their bout and felt he wasn't skilled enough to hang with Royce, despite the very deep competitive résumé Yoshida brought to the table.

Frye and Yoshida battled at PRIDE 23 on November 24, 2002. North American fans expected Frye, still undefeated in PRIDE under mixed martial arts rules, to make quick work of the phony Yoshida. Frye expected the same thing, and he took Yoshida lightly going into the fight. Fans were in disbelief when Yoshida made very quick work of Frye, putting him on his back and eventually locking in an armbar to get the referee to stop the fight at 5:32 because, despite the massive amount of pain from the hold, Don Frye would not give up (simply because he's Don Frye and giving up is not in his vocabulary).

Many, if not most, North American MMA fans didn't buy into the idea that Yoshida could possibly have defeated someone of Don Frye's caliber. Because Don Frye had worked for so many years as a pro wrestler, fans felt that the bout must have been a work—even though the armbar that Frye had refused to submit to had dislocated his elbow, which he would later need surgery for. Frye had also aggravated a bad neck injury in the fight.

Frye had a new respect for Yoshida after the fight. "He's the most decorated athlete to come into MMA," said Frye in an interview with PRIDE. "Being the most decorated athlete, he's at the top of his level. He's not going to
come in and start at the bottom. I really respect him. I'm glad he gave me the
opportunity to fight him."

"Everyone says that he's a rookie, but he's not a rookie," Frye stated in
an interview with PRIDE. "The guy had two or three thousand matches plus
training eight hours a day for many years. There's no rookie aspect about him.
He's ready to go. He's a trained professional."

Frye's body was falling apart at this point. His last four fights against
Yoshida, LeBanner, Takayama, and Ken Shamrock had really taken a toll on
him, and physically he just wasn't the same fighter that he once had been.
Frye didn't have time to worry about this, though, because he was preparing
to finally avenge the first and only loss for many years of his MMA career by
taking on Mark Coleman at PRIDE 26 on June 8, 2003.

Coleman hadn't fought in MMA since his loss to Antonio Rodrigo
Nogueira on September 24, 2001, and he had gone through a divorce during this period of time. It was unclear how well he would do against Frye, as
Frye had been competing far more regularly but was far more beat up, and
in reality, not much had changed with the two fighters since the last time
they met many years earlier, except that they were now both a lot older and
somewhat wiser.

The first Coleman-Frye fight, at UFC 10, had been a classic war between a
larger and more dangerous opponent and his foe, Frye, who simply wouldn't
give up in the face of disaster. The second bout was a much slower affair, as
Coleman managed to put Frye down on the ground and slowly pounded him
to win a decision victory. The fight was a disappointment for Frye, as not only
was he unable to get revenge against Coleman, but the fight was considered
dull. Frye had gone from being undefeated in PRIDE to losing three in a row
under MMA and K-1 rules.

The final fight on Frye's contract with PRIDE at the time came on New Year's Eve 2003. His opponent was Gary Goodridge, who had stepped away from MMA for a while due to custody issues with one of his children. PRIDE let Goodridge select any opponent he wanted for his "retirement" match. He chose Frye.

December 31, 2003, was the biggest one-night business war in the history of the industry, as PRIDE, K-1, and Antonio Inoki were all running major stadium shows that aired on network television on the same night at the same time. Nearly everyone who was anyone in the world of MMA was involved in these shows, and then some.

Frye versus Goodridge would, of course, take place on the PRIDE card. Goodridge sought to avenge his two prior losses to Frye years earlier in UFC. Surprising everyone and showing how broken-down Frye was at that point in his career, Goodridge succeeded, knocking Frye out with a kick to the head thirty-nine seconds into the fight. Goodridge was never known for his kickboxing skills, and he shocked the world by defeating Don Frye so quickly. Although Frye had been beaten up badly in the past, this was the first time he was knocked out under MMA rules.

If someone of Don Frye's charisma, looks, and abilities came along today at the heavyweight level, he'd be a superstar. "Frye was a guy where he got on the screen and people just started watching," says promoter and broadcaster Jeff Osborne. One of the most charismatic fighters ever in MMA, Frye always has a funny answer to any question. When asked by an interviewer from PRIDE how long he's had his trademark mustache, Frye replied, "Since I was five. I got it from my mom's side of the family. She's not a pretty woman."

Frye is also known as one of the nicest fighters outside the ring. "Not only are you representing yourself but also your sport and the promoters," he said in an interview with *Pride FC* about fighting in MMA. "You want to represent them properly. You just don't want to give anything a black eye. I think that's the way professionals should conduct themselves. Especially, the way they treat the fans. I mean, you see these baseball players making millions of dollars, and then they've got to charge the fans twenty dollars for an autograph. There's not reason for that."

Don Frye is clearly in the December of his career. He's been working in pro wrestling off and on throughout his run in PRIDE, including a tag team match with Ken Shamrock against Keiji Mutoh and Nobuhiko Takada headlining the December 31, 2000, Inoki Bom Ba Ye event at the Osaka Dome in front of over 42,000 people. Whether he goes back to pro wrestling full-time or tries to break his losing streak in MMA is anyone's guess. Knowing Frye's never-give-up attitude and his headstrong way of taking a fight no matter what obstacles or supposedly handicapping injuries he might face, the answer should be an obvious one.

Mark Coleman

Mark Coleman represents the pinnacle of power wrestling in mixed martial arts. Nicknamed "The Hammer" because of his size and strength, Coleman combines these assets with his amazing wrestling skills to throw his opponents to the canvas and beat them like tent poles. It may sound like a simple strategy, but it has brought Coleman to the peak of MMA: his accomplishments include holding the UFC Heavyweight title and winning the 2000 PRIDE Grand Prix tournament.

Coleman was born on December 20, 1964, and grew up in a small town called Fremont, two hours north of Columbus, Ohio. A natural athlete, the young Coleman played baseball, football, and wrestled at Fremont St. Joseph's, the Catholic high school he attended as a teenager.

Coleman ended up at Miami of Ohio University on a baseball scholarship, but as a junior at the school in 1986, he also placed fourth in the NCAA Division I 190-lb. weight division in wrestling.

Coleman transferred to Ohio State as a senior, and in 1988 he placed first in the NCAA Division I 190-lb. weight division, capping off his college wrestling success. He graduated from Ohio State with a degree in education.

"I pursued the goal of being a world champion, and an Olympic champion in wrestling, and in 1991, I won the Pan American games gold medal in Cuba," says Coleman in an interview for Sherdog.com. "Then I won the United States National Freestyle championships, and went on to the World championships where I took a silver medal. I hadn't lost in six tournaments during the 1991–92 season."

Coleman went on to compete in the '92 Summer Olympics in Barcelona. He was a top seed going into the competition. He made the Olympic team at 220 pounds, but had a disappointing outing in the Olympics, and would end placing seventh despite the fact that he was figured to have done much better.

Coleman floated around for the next few years, competing in amateur wrestling and aiming for another shot at the Olympics in 1996, although during that time he did little training.

In 1995, Coleman competed in the Sunkist Open Tournament, where he defeated future Olympic gold medalist and pro wrestler Kurt Angle; then he took his shot at making the Olympics in '96. He ended up losing in the semifinals of the Olympic qualifier. This was the last time Coleman made a run at Olympic competition.

Even though Coleman didn't make it back to the Olympics, trainer Richard Hamilton approached him at the Olympic trials. Hamilton was scouting Coleman as well as Tom Erikson and Mark Kerr (amateur wrestlers who would both go on to have successful careers in MMA) to compete for him in UFC 10, which would take place just thirty days later on July 12, 1996.

Coleman took Hamilton up on the offer, and when he walked out to the octagon for his first UFC match, Coleman was pretty much a pure freestyle wrestler with only thirty days of hard training in submission grappling and striking.

Coleman's first opponent in the one-night UFC 10 was a karate practitioner named Moti Horenstein. Coleman took Horenstein down right out of the gate, quickly proceeded to get full mount, then pounded his opponent into submission at 2:43. Coleman won his MMA debut, and the fight began his mixed martial arts legacy, ushering in a new style of fighting that involved muscular wrestlers using their strength and skills to put an opponent on the ground and simply hammer him.

The fight also sent Coleman into the second round of the tournament, where he met the charismatic Gary "Big Daddy" Goodridge. Goodridge had been a runner-up in the UFC 8 tournament months earlier and, much like Coleman, would become an even bigger star in MMA in Japan. Coleman took Goodridge down immediately, but Goodridge ended up back on his feet, trying to knock Coleman out. When that didn't happen, Coleman took Goodridge down again and was able to get a mount, but Goodridge gave up at 7:00, figuring there was nothing more he could do.

Coleman was now in the UFC 10 tournament finals, despite it being his very first night competing in mixed martial arts. His opponent was the tough and highly skilled Don Frye, who had won the UFC 8 tournament and who later went on to win the second Ultimate Ultimate tournament in December of 1996. Although Frye was outsized by Coleman, he was the favorite to win the fight going in because of his experience in UFC.

Coleman versus Frye went down as one of the most exciting and most brutal fights from that era in UFC, as Coleman made an everlasting mark on the promotion when he gave Frye the thrashing of his life en route to handing him his first-ever loss in mixed martial arts.

Coleman managed to close both of Frye's eyes and opened a cut on him serious enough that referee John McCarthy stopped the fight to check it. When the fight was restarted, Coleman continued to beat on Frye, ferociously slamming him back down to the canvas. Coleman continued to punish Frye on the ground, and eventually, at 11:34, the fight was stopped. Coleman was the UFC 10 tournament champion, and not only had he defeated Don Frye, one of the very best UFC fighters of that time, but he had also given him an absolute beating.

"When I won UFC 10, I was overwhelmed. That was something that really I only dreamed about, being the toughest man in the world," says Coleman in the Sherdog.com interview. "Even in boxing, you can be the toughest boxer in the world, but being the toughest man is something you can kind of brag about. When I won the UFC, I felt like I was the toughest man in the world, it was overwhelming." Years later, in PRIDE, Frye and Coleman met again in a very different rematch, but with a similar result.

Now a bona fide star with the promotion, Coleman returned to the UFC at their very next event, the one-night UFC 11 tournament on September 20, 1996. On the opposite end of the brackets was Tank Abbott, returning from a lengthy suspension from UFC. Fans were anxiously awaiting the Tank versus Coleman matchup in the finals.

Coleman's first-round opponent was Julian Sanchez. Coleman took care of him with a choke in forty-five seconds, and sent himself into the semifinals. Elsewhere in the first round, Tank Abbott used a neck crank to submit Sam Adkins. In the second round, Coleman was able to submit Brian Johnston by nailing him with a series of punishing strikes from within Johnston's half guard at only 2:20. The win launched him into the finals of the tournament.

However, in the other semifinals fight, Tank Abbott came up against the obese Scott Ferrozzo, and surprisingly, Ferrozzo, then a training partner of Don Frye's, defeated Tank Abbott by decision in a long fight, axing any chance of seeing Tank versus Coleman in the tournament finals. Unfortunately, Ferrozzo didn't end up fighting either, as he pulled out of the tournament due to exhaustion from his long battle against Tank. The alternate for the tournament also bowed out, claiming an injury and perhaps just not wanting to face Coleman's vicious onslaught. Coleman was left with no opponent. In a strange ending to the pay-per-view, there was no tournament final, and Coleman was simply brought out to the octagon and hailed as the tournament champion. Although this win was a little hollow, Coleman had now won his second UFC tournament in a row.

His next battle in the octagon was scheduled for the 1996 Ultimate Ultimate tournament, which was to be loaded with top fighters and which Coleman would have been a strong favorite to win, despite the fact that the tournament featured other top fighters such as Frye, Ken Shamrock, and Tank Abbott. However, thyroid problems kept Coleman out of the tournament and out of the octagon for a few months.

He made his return on February 7, 1997, at UFC 12. There he had his chance to fight for what was the pinnacle of UFC competition at the time, taking on UFC Superfight champion Dan Severn for the title.

Severn had fallen out of favor with UFC's parent company, SEG, following his poor performance at UFC 9, even though he had defeated Ken Shamrock to win the belt. SEG had decided not to book him again, despite the fact he was the company's champion, until they booked him in this fight against Coleman, a fight that many people—including Severn himself—didn't think he had much of a chance to win.

First, though, Coleman fired his trainer and manager, Richard Hamilton, the man who had discovered him at the Olympic trials in 1996, when Hamilton's shady past came to light. Coleman and Hamilton had a falling out, and their manager-fighter relationship was over.

Going up against Severn, Coleman's fighting style seemed unbeatable. The style was simple: Coleman used the huge power and size advantage he had over most of his opponents and combined it with his superior wrestling skills to easily take opponents down to the canvas and simply pummel them into submission, or finish them with an easy submission, such as a side choke or a neck crank. This style became known as "ground-and-pound," and paved the way for many other successful power wrestlers using this technique to make it to the top of the mixed martial arts world. "I feel I invented the ground-and-pound, and some people have me confused with the ground and hold," says Coleman in his interview with Sherdog.com. "I have to do what I do best, and that's take people to the ground, and I don't hold on, I try to pound them."

Although Severn was also a top-tier former amateur wrestler (Severn had been a top wrestler in college in the early '80s, whereas Coleman's star rose in the late '80s), Coleman's power was unmatched. Coleman had problems going into the fight with taking on another amateur wrestler, as fighters with similar styles at times didn't want to be matched against one another.

Any emotional objection he had to fighting Severn faded, however, once the bout was under way. Coleman was quickly able to get a full mount on Severn and submit him with a neck crank at only 2:57. It was Severn's last UFC appearance for many years. Not only had Coleman captured the UFC Superfight championship, but, as the reigning UFC Heavyweight tournament champion and having just won the Superfight title, he was also awarded the UFC Heavyweight title, which made him technically the first Heavyweight champion in UFC history.

Coleman's first defense of the UFC Heavyweight title would be against Extreme Fighting Heavyweight champion Maurice Smith at UFC 14 on July 27, 1997. UFC 12 had been the last UFC event on cable under the ownership of SEG, as mixed martial arts had been placed under a cable ban. Other groups, such as Extreme Fighting, had simply gone out of business, and many of their fighters jumped over to UFC. Smith was one of them.

Smith, one of the top kickboxers of the 1980s, had captured the Extreme Fighting Heavyweight championship by training in cardio and in groundfighting with Frank Shamrock, then defeating Conan Silveira in the finals of a tournament to win the title. Smith had continued to train with Shamrock for the fight against Coleman. Generally, when a kickboxer comes up against a grappler, the kickboxer will lose. But this time was different. The outcome of the bout was a major surprise, and went down as one of the biggest upsets in MMA history.

Coleman was undefeated in UFC at this point. Not only had he defeated many of the other top UFC fighters of the time, like Frye and Severn, he had walked through them, and in the process, he looked unbeatable. He didn't take Smith seriously going into this fight, and instead of training, he spent his time partying, not paying attention to the fact that he could lose his Heavyweight title in his very first defense of the belt.

Coleman figured that he would simply take the kickboxer down to the canvas and either pound him into submission or tap him out with a neck crank or a choke. And when the fight started that night in Birmingham, Alabama, it seemed that it would go that way, as Coleman immediately managed to take Smith down to the ground. Coleman was even able to get full mount on the ground initially, but Smith's training in groundfighting with Shamrock foiled any plans to either pound him or submit him, and Coleman wasn't able to do anything in the mount.

By partying and not training, Coleman had destroyed any chance he might have had at winning a long fight, as he gassed out quickly and lacked the energy to seriously go the distance in the bout. "After the two-minute mark," he says, "everything fell into place, and I realized how dumb I was for taking on a championship fighter of Maurice Smith's caliber and just absolutely showing him no respect." As the fight wore on, Coleman didn't press the action, and kept resting his hands on his knees, looking very tired. Despite his fatigue, his amazing wrestling skills carried him through to the end of the fight, and even late in the bout, he was able to take Smith down to the canvas, but he was so tired and weak that he wasn't able to keep the kickboxer there. "I didn't quit," says Coleman. "I was still going for the win."

After two three-minute overtime periods, Coleman was completely and totally spent, even though he had a rest between each period. The fight went to a decision, which Smith, of course, won. "Mark took the fight lightly and paid dearly for it," says John McCarthy, who refereed the bout. "Not many people thought Mo had a chance against Mark."

In losing his Heavyweight title to Smith, both a newcomer and a striker, Coleman learned a valuable lesson about not being too confident of his own skills, a lesson that would help him at a later point in his career.

Coleman's next fight, against Lion's Den trainee Pete Williams, reaffirmed that lesson. Coleman had taken a few months off because he had injured his ACL, and, wanting to prove that his loss to Smith was a mere fluke, he returned from his ACL surgery much too fast.

On May 15, 1998, at UFC 17, Williams knocked Coleman out at 12:38 of the fight with an infamous highlight reel–style kick to the head that put Coleman to sleep. It was now two losses in a row for the former two-time UFC tournament and one-time Heavyweight champion.

Determined to prove himself, and to discredit those two straight losses, Coleman returned to the octagon for UFC 18 a few months later, on January 8, 1999. There he took on the dangerous up-and-coming striker Pedro Rizzo.

It was a very close fight, split between the ground and standup action. The fighters were also restarted at one point in the bout due to lack of action. It ended up going to the judges, and Rizzo won via a controversial split-decision. "I clearly thought I won that fight. It was not one of my better fights; it was at a time when I didn't know that much about fighting. I kind of winged it, and I got through with my athletic ability," Coleman admits to Sherdog. com. "I really didn't know much about the standup game, or about the guard. I had to be very careful; I was coming off of two losses. I really wasn't in the best shape of my life, so I did what I had to do. Normally I go out there to win, and to entertain the crowd, because that's critical. If you don't entertain the crowd and you win, it doesn't do anybody any good. But this time I just needed a win, so I was out there trying for a win."

The loss against Rizzo was Coleman's final fight in UFC as, although he had once been a seemingly unbeatable fighter with an undefeated record, he was now on a streak of three straight losses. Coleman signed a deal with PRIDE to go over and fight in Japan. "If Coleman's career would have ended after his losses in the UFC to Smith, Pedro Rizzo, and especially when he was knocked out by Pete Williams, it would have hurt his standing in the history of the sport," says Stephen Quadros. "But he came around and diversified his training, which caused him to rise to the top of the sport again after he left the UFC."

Coleman's debut with PRIDE took place on April 29, 1999, at PRIDE 5 against Nobuhiko Takada—a huge superstar in Japan who had name value from his years as a headliner in pro wrestling but who was ultimately a terrible fighter—in a fight that many people suspect was a work to give Takada a win over a big-name fighter. Coleman lost to Takada at 1:44 of the second round via submission from a heel hook. Coleman claims that the fight was real despite the fact he lost it, and whether or not the fight was fixed, it went down as a fourth straight loss on Coleman's record, although because of the controversy of it possibly being a work, it's a loss many feel doesn't count.

At this point, although he was fighting in PRIDE, which was quickly becoming one of the premier promotions in Japan, Coleman's stock had sunk. PRIDE decided that, in his next fight, which would take place at PRIDE 8 on November 21, 1999, he would face the 6'8", 270-lb Ricardo Morais.

Coleman was an underdog going in against the gigantic Morais, who had only lost once in his career (via decision) at that point. Coleman's bout against Morais was slow, but in the end he was able to go the distance and win a decision. It was Coleman's first victory in nearly three years.

The next portion of Coleman's career was arguably the most important: in 2000, PRIDE decided to run their first Grand Prix tournament. Coleman was entered in the first round.

At the time, it was hard to say how well Coleman would do in the tournament, as he hadn't defeated a really high-level fighter in years at that point, and mixed martial arts had changed drastically while Coleman was on his losing streak. One of the biggest changes in MMA, a change that would hurt Coleman's offensive tactics, was the elimination of headbutts. Coleman was known to use devastating headbutts as a part of his ground-and-pound strategy.

Nevertheless, Coleman was in the tournament, and had to find a way to win to silence his critics and prove himself a top heavyweight fighter in MMA. The opening round of the tournament took place on January 20, 2000, at the

Tokyo Dome. The winners of each fight would go on to compete in the rest of the tournament later that year.

Coleman's first-round opponent was former karate star and K-1 competitor Masaaki Satake, a fighter who had limited skill and experience in mixed martial arts. Since Satake was mainly a striker and Coleman was mainly a wrestler, it appeared that Coleman would make quick work of the Japanese striker. And he did, taking Satake down to the canvas and submitting him with a neck crank in only 1:14.

The win advanced Coleman to the second night of the tournament, also at the Tokyo Dome, on May 1, 2000. His opponent: the wily and underrated Akira Shoji. To win the tournament, Coleman would have to defeat Shoji, and then go through two more fighters later in the night. Since Coleman had a reputation for gassing out in his fights, it seemed unlikely that he'd be able to fight that often in one night and not get tired. Plus with other highly skilled fighters, such as Mark Kerr, Royce Gracie, Kazushi Sakuraba, and Igor Vovchanchyn, still in the tournament, the odds seemed stacked against Coleman's success.

The fight against Shoji ended up going really well for Coleman, and really badly for Shoji. Coleman seemed to have improved his standup game, and he dominated Shoji to win a decision.

One fight down, two to go for the former UFC champion that night. A lucky break came up for Coleman, though, in the third round of the tournament—his second fight of the night. Kazuyuki Fujita, a highly skilled Japanese heavyweight fighter, had upset one of the tournament favorites, the enigmatic Mark Kerr, earlier in the night, but was injured during the fight. Fujita's third-round opponent was, of course, Coleman, and Fujita's corner ended up throwing in the towel right at the start of the fight. It was a fluke, to be sure, but partially due to that fluke, Mark Coleman found himself in the finals of the biggest tournament up to that point in MMA history.

His opponent for the finals was the very dangerous striker Igor

Vovchanchyn, who had gone through lengthy fights with Gary Goodridge and Kazushi Sakuraba earlier in the night and wasn't as well rested heading into the match as Coleman was.

Coleman and Vovchanchyn battled it out throughout the first round of the fight and into the second. Vovchanchyn was clearly tired and Coleman, who'd been on an easier path to the finals, looked rested. At 3:09 of the second round, Vovchanchyn gave up after Coleman pulverized him with seventeen knees to his head. Coleman had defeated Igor Vovchanchyn to win the PRIDE Grand Prix, and was ecstatic, leaping around the ring like a maniac, then jumping into the crowd, where he nearly bulldozed over some ringside spectators.

It was a huge victory for Coleman, easily the biggest of his career. Not only had he won the $200,000 tournament prize, not only had he won the biggest and most difficult mixed martial arts tournament up to that point in time, but he had also won back the respect of everyone in the MMA world after years of looking like a second-class fighter. Once again, Mark Coleman was the top heavyweight fighter on the planet.

After the Grand Prix victory, Coleman took some time off. He returned at PRIDE 13 on March 25, 2001, to take on the tough Allan Goes at the Saitama Super Arena. In an amusing and somewhat strange ceremony before the fight, pro wrestling icon and then–PRIDE power broker Antonio Inoki came out and claimed that the fight would be for the WWF World Martial Arts title belt, a pro wrestling title that was used by New Japan Pro Wrestling, a promotion Inoki himself had run from 1978 to 1992. In the fight itself, Coleman quickly took Goes down to the canvas and destroyed him with knees until the referee stepped in and stopped the fight at 1:19. Coleman was subsequently awarded the pro wrestling title.

The world of mixed martial arts is a funny one. For years, Coleman was considered an unbeatable premier fighter in the sport, and then for a number of years after that, he was seen as washed up and unable to win a fight, but after winning the PRIDE Grand Prix and disposing of Goes so quickly, Coleman again looked unbeatable.

But every superman has his kryptonite, and Coleman's next opponent, Antonio Rodrigo Nogueira, the best submissions grappler at the heavyweight level in MMA, would be Coleman's kryptonite.

Nogueira versus Coleman took place at PRIDE 16 on September 24, 2001. It was the battle of the violent power wrestler against the skilled submissions master, the two of them arguably considered the best heavyweight fighters on the planet at the time.

Nogueira won the fight standing, and when it went to the ground, he used an armbar to quickly submit Coleman at 6:10 into the match. With the exception of the controversial Nobuhiko Takada fight, it was the first time Coleman had ever been tapped out in a fight, despite the fact that many feel Coleman's submissions defense has never evolved with the times in MMA.

Coleman took a leave of absence from the world of mixed martial arts. He was booked to come back and fight Don Frye at PRIDE in 2002 in a rematch of their heavy-hitting bout from UFC 10 years earlier, but Coleman was injured before the fight could take place, and had to pull out. Yoshihiro Takayama took his place, and Don Frye laid a violent beating on him to win that fight.

Coleman and Frye did meet, however, at PRIDE 26 on June 8, 2003. Frye had wanted this rematch badly for many years since, for a very long time, Coleman was the only fighter to have ever defeated him in MMA. Having recently lost to Hidehiko Yoshida, and also to Jerome LeBanner under K-1 rules, Frye was looking for redemption. Absent from the MMA scene for nearly two years, Coleman had a lot to prove.

The first fight between Coleman and Frye in UFC had been an exciting and devastating war. Although this fight had all the same ingredients, it was a disappointment in comparison to the previous fight. Coleman used his size advantage, combined with his amazing wrestling skills, to take Frye down and keep him on the canvas, slowly pounding him to a dull decision victory. Other than the victory, the only positive that came out of the fight for Coleman was that, despite having taken nearly two years off from MMA competition, he hadn't gassed out when going the distance against Frye, which could have been a problem for the former Olympian.

Back in shape and back in the MMA ring after having overcome some personal problems in his marriage and having surgery on his neck, Coleman's career was about to come full circle. PRIDE had run another Grand Prix in 2003 for middleweight fighters only, which was won by PRIDE Middleweight champion Wanderlei Silva. The promotion decided to go back to the original heavyweight format of the Grand Prix in 2004, and so Coleman, the Grand Prix champion from 2000, was invited back to the tournament, the first round of which took place on April 25, 2004.

Despite his rapidly advancing age and his time away from the sport, not to mention the fact that he hadn't fought a top guy in his prime since losing to Nogueira in 2001, Coleman was favored by many to win his first-round fight. The fight was against the promotion's Heavyweight champion, the Russian monster Fedor Emelianenko, who was unbeaten in PRIDE competition and nearly flawless as a fighter, if such a thing is possible. Coleman would be a tough opponent for Fedor, however, because his power and skills would likely enable him to take Fedor down to the canvas and pound him to a ref stoppage or a decision victory.

"I want to show everyone that the champion is still alive," said Coleman before the fight in an interview with PRIDE. "I haven't been able to practice well for the last three years because of my neck injury. It bothered me in fights, too. I had surgery six months ago, though, and I've been training well since. It's not just a restarting point for me. I think this match will be bigger than that."

But whether it was Coleman's age, his time away from the ring, or the fact that MMA had advanced beyond his skills, he could no longer hang with the very top heavyweight fighters, and the victory would not be his. Despite taking Fedor down and putting him on his back, Coleman was submitted just 2:11 into the fight with an armbar. The defending heavyweight Grand Prix tournament champion had just lost his bid to make it into the second round of the 2004 tournament.

It's hard to say what the future holds for Mark Coleman. He started to slowly branch out into pro wrestling in Japan at the start of the millennium, and seems to be a natural at it; despite being basically a novice in the medium, his athletic gifts make for high-quality matches. He plans to continue to fight for PRIDE. Even as he approaches the age of forty, it's still too soon to rule out a comeback: Coleman has bounced back from very bad defeats before, and it's certainly within the realm of possibility that he could do so again.

Frank Juarez Shamrock

Frank Shamrock is the definition of the cerebral mixed martial arts athlete. He was the bridge between the Royce Gracie era of UFC, with looser and far fewer rules, and the modern era of UFC and mixed martial arts. Frank brought cardio conditioning, intelligent strategy, and cross-training between many forms of fighting to the forefront of the sport, and was one of the only stars during UFC's biggest down period.

Shamrock was born Frank Alicio Juarez III on December 8, 1972, in Santa Monica, California. His early childhood years were difficult. "My dad left when, I think, I was three. Three or four. I had seen him off and on for the next few years, then he disappeared completely," recalls Frank in an interview with Mike Sloan for Sherdog.com. "So I didn't have a Dad and I was running around as this wild kid with brown, long hair. Mom was trying to take care of us. There was four of us and her. I grew up that way not as a young man, but as a kid.

"Then when I was about seven or eight, my Mom met her boyfriend and everything changed," Frank continues. "It was different. He was strict, he was militant, he was totally different and it didn't make sense to me. I couldn't figure out what was wrong with me. I ended up leaving my home when I was twelve years old and going into the system, going into the state. And once I got into the system, it was all downhill from there."

Frank was moved from foster home to group home to crisis center to juvenile hall and back around again in the California foster care system. Eventually,

Bob Shamrock invited Frank to come stay at his group home for young boys, the Shamrock Ranch in Susanville, California. Shamrock had raised countless other boys there, including the first famous mixed martial artist to take on Bob's name, Ken Shamrock. Ken was years older than Frank, and although the two of them are the most famous people bearing the Shamrock name, they're not tremendously close to each other.

Ken eventually broke into pro wrestling in the late 1980s, and at that point, he and Bob moved to North Carolina, where Ken could advance his training in the sports entertainment industry. As a result, Bob closed the Shamrock Ranch for a period of time. Frank, who was sixteen at the time, went back through the circuit of California foster homes. He eventually returned to Susanville, where he impregnated his high-school girlfriend. Frank decided to marry her before he was even seventeen, and this made him an adult in the eyes of the California government. While he continued to get his high-school education, Frank also took on two jobs to support his new family.

Frank eventually wound up in jail and divorced. At this point, Bob Shamrock had moved back to California, and the local sheriff allowed him to visit Frank every other week in jail. When the twenty-one-year-old Frank was released on April 4, 1994, he moved in with Bob, who legally adopted him. Although Ken and Frank had never been very close while they lived together at the Shamrock Ranch, the very next day in Lodi, California, Frank started to train under Ken in submission fighting.

"I saw the fight as being the story, and I didn't want to participate because I didn't really like the violence," said Frank in an interview conducted for this book. "What I liked and what I appreciated was the athleticism, the courage, and the sacrifice. To be perfectly honest, I didn't really want to do it."

Frank was one of the first members of the Lion's Den, the original stable of mixed martial artists put together to help Ken Shamrock prepare for his fights. The Lion's Den would grow to be a highly influential model for how fighters could team together to train and share knowledge. Frank also started to accompany Ken to his UFC fights. He trained for seven months at the Lion's Den in Lodi, before, like all other fighters who trained with the Lion's Den, he was sent to Japan to train at Pancrase's dojo, Kanagawa Ku, for six weeks. Frank, who initially fought as Frank Juarez but later took on the name Frank Shamrock, made his fighting debut with Pancrase in the first round of the King of Pancrase title tournament on December 16, 1994, taking on the charismatic Dutch kickboxer and budding submissions expert Bas Rutten.

Despite the fact that Bas broke Frank's nose with a kick during the fight, Frank was able to take Rutten to the ground, where he was most comfortable, and went the full distance in the ten-minute-long fight, defeating Bas by majority decision. "It was very strange to me," says Frank. "The bell rang, there was lots of moving around, and then the bell rang again. To me it seemed like it was two minutes long!"

The win launched Frank into the second round of the tournament later in the night, where he was submitted by Manabu Yamada, who then went on to the finals the next night and was defeated by Ken at 8:38. Frank had made it to the quarterfinals of the tournament that would decide the first King of Pancrase, and this began to establish him as a new legend in MMA. "I won the first fight [against Rutten], [and] he was ranked number three at the time," says Frank. "And that immediately pushed me into the superstar status, and it just took off from there."

Frank returned to the Pancrase ring on January 26, 1995, submitting Katsuomi Inagaki at 6:14. This win would lead Shamrock to a fight with Pancrase star Masakatsu Funaki on March 10, 1995, where Frank suffered his second loss, submitted by Funaki at 5:11. Undaunted, Frank came back from this loss by submitting another major star of Pancrase, Minoru Suzuki, one of the best in Pancrase in that early era, on April 8, 1995, at 3:23. Frank was quickly becoming a submissions master, and although his kickboxing skill at the time was very poor (he had basically only trained in submissions), his submissions had to have developed rapidly to submit a fighter of Suzuki's caliber that quickly.

On May 13, 1995, Shamrock came up against the toughest opponent of his career up to that point: Allan Goes. After having fought in Pancrase, Frank had the mind-set that the Japanese fighters were the pinnacle of the sport and everyone else should be disregarded, and since Goes was Brazilian and not Japanese, Frank underestimated his competitor as he went into the fight. He even drank and smoked weed the night before the fight.

The fight was a war. "I was just an athlete competing in a sport, and I didn't understand the need to create and inflict damage—the mental strength that it takes, not only to hurt people, but to be willing to accept the punishment," says Frank. Well, Frank would come to understand the mental strength required to both take damage and dish it out when he fought Goes as, despite a gentleman's rule in place at the time in Pancrase forbidding strikes to a downed opponent, Goes made sure to hit Frank in the head when he was on the ground.

Each fighter had a rope break during the fight, and although Frank had actually broken Goes's leg, the bout went ten minutes before it went to the judges' table. It was ruled a draw in the end. "That match taught me that there was a difference between sport and fighting, and I had a brief taste of it," says Frank.

Shamrock would use this new insight to advance himself another step, always looking for a way to better himself as a competitor. He returned to Pancrase a month later with a win, submitting Takaku Fuke at 8:16 on June 13, 1995. His next fight, however, was a loss, as he was rematched with the much-improved Bas Rutten on July 23, 1995, and Frank ended up on the short end of a close split-decision after the fight went its distance of fifteen minutes. Undaunted, Frank Shamrock returned with a six-fight winning streak, which lasted from when he submitted Takafumi Ito on September 1, 1995, at Sumo Hall to when he defeated Osami Shibuya via decision on April 8, 1996, at Korakuen Hall. In late 1995, Shamrock also submitted fellow Lion's Den trainee Vernon White and avenged his loss against Masakatsu Funaki by submitting him with a toe hold.

During the six-fight winning streak, Frank's best run in Pancrase, he captured the provisional King of Pancrase title—the same title he'd competed for on his debut night with the promotion. Bas Rutten, who had defeated Minoru Suzuki for the title in September 1995, was injured, so the plan was for Frank Shamrock to fight Suzuki to declare an interim champion until Rutten was healthy. When Frank and Minoru met for the second time of their careers on January 28, 1996, Frank held one win over Suzuki from their April 1995 fight. Once again, Frank defeated Suzuki via submission, and won the provisional championship.

"I was athletic, but I never competed in any sports, I wasn't on any team, I was just athletic," said Frank about his quick success in MMA in an interview for RealFighting.com. "But I never envisioned myself doing anything like this, and I never had any martial arts training, and I was never a street fighter."

Before defending the provisional King of Pancrase title in a unification match with Bas Rutten on May 16, 1996, Frank defeated Ryushi Yanagisawa via decision on March 2, 1996, and also decisioned Osamu Shibuya on April 8, 1996. Rutten and Shamrock, of course, each held one victory over the other from earlier on, but Rutten had continued to improve so greatly as a mixed martial artist that by the time of their rubber match he was in the midst of a four-year-long undefeated streak in MMA.

"Several minutes into the fight, I realized that Bas was just too strong for me and that I wasn't going to make the time limit and be able to finesse him into a hold," says Frank when interviewed for this book. At this point in the bout, Frank figured that the only way he could win the fight was by getting Rutten to foul against him. "In my twisted little mind, I thought I could create a foul by making him angry, and Bas gets angered easily," says Frank. "I knew if I got him angry that he would eventually hit me with a closed fist, and I would get a point."

In a classic scene in mixed martial arts, as Rutten and Frank were dueling on the ground over leglocks, Frank actually stuck his tongue out at the Dutch fighter and made funny faces at him, trying to anger him. The strategy failed, though, as Rutten was eventually able to open a cut on Frank with a knee, and the cut was bad enough that it ended the fight. Frank had lost his provisional King of Pancrase championship belt.

Frank came back from that loss to submit Manabu Yamada, who had defeated Frank on Frank's first night in Pancrase. After this, however, Frank suffered two consecutive losses in Pancrase: the first on September 7, 1996, knocked out by Yuki Kondo; and, in the final fight of his career in Pancrase, on December 15, 1996, when Kiuma Kunioku defeated Frank via decision.

At that time, problems with Pancrase and Ken Shamrock began to crop up, generating a lot of heat and negative feelings between Pancrase and the Shamrock party. Ken left Pancrase, and subsequently the promotion didn't treat Frank very well.

"I didn't know what I wanted to, do so I was just going over there and collecting a paycheck," says Frank. "Ken left, and there were some legal dealings that made me uncomfortable. Pancrase accused me of doing steroids, and things became unpleasant."

Frank and Pancrase parted ways after his loss to Kunioku. This was one in a series of changes in the life and career of Frank Shamrock during this time. In 1996, Ken Shamrock had become friends with Maurice Smith, a kickboxer who had also competed in Pancrase in the early '90s. Through that friendship with Ken, Maurice also linked up with Frank Shamrock. Frank and Maurice's friendship and the time they spent training together would prove to be very influential to the future development of mixed martial arts. Frank and Maurice's partnership worked out well because Smith was a poor grappler and Shamrock was a poor striker.

"I was a terrible striker, and Maurice was a so-so grappler," says Shamrock. Essentially, Smith trained with Frank Shamrock, teaching Frank everything he knew about striking to improve Frank's standup game, and in turn Frank taught Smith everything he knew about grappling.

Frank helped Smith prepare for his debut North American MMA rules fight at Extreme Challenge 3 in October 1996 against jiu jitsu expert Conan Silveira by working on Smith's groundfighting game. Smith used his newly acquired skills to defeat Silveira in Extreme Fighting, then defeated Kazunari Murakami in March 1997 to become the first Extreme Fighting Heavyweight champion. His new skills in fighting on the ground took Smith a long way. Without Shamrock's help, Smith would never have gone so far in that promotion, and he certainly wouldn't have defeated Silveira.

Shamrock also made his North American MMA debut during this period of time, signing on to fight John Lober at SuperBrawl 3 in Hawaii on January 17, 1997. It was also to be the first closed-fist fight of Frank's career, since his entire career up to that point had been in Pancrase, which of course banned closed fists at that time.

Frank considers this fight to be the true beginning of his mixed martial arts career, and the moment when he started to take off as a legend in the sport. "When I fought Lober, I found a guy who wasn't going to get tired. He wasn't going to give up," says Frank in his interview with Mike Sloan. "And he didn't care if I broke something, so I had to condition myself not to care. I had to tell myself, 'It's okay if he gets hurt, if he's trying to hurt me.' And once I made that decision I never looked back. I changed how I viewed the art."

The fight with Lober was a thirty-minute war. Lober just kept coming at Frank during the entire thirty-minute fight, and Frank walked away on the losing end of a very close split-decision.

Not only did Shamrock improve as a fighter, but his understanding of what draws money in MMA also grew. "Most [fighters], like I did, only want to perfect the art and could really care less about the entertainment," said Shamrock in an interview for this book. "I was really blessed that I grew up [as a fighter] in Japan, where you are judged on your entertainment value."

On July 14, 1997, Shamrock competed on a pay-per-view event called The Contenders, backed by USA Wrestling, and featuring submissions-only bouts between highly skilled submission fighters and amateur wrestlers. Shamrock's opponent was Dan Henderson, whom Shamrock submitted with an ankle lock in just fifty-six seconds. Henderson would later go on to become one of the top fighters in mixed martial arts. As an event, however, The Contenders failed, due to lack of fan interest.

After losing to Lober and defeating Dan Henderson, Frank returned to the Japanese fight world in September 1997, this time not with Pancrase, but with RINGS, a company that promoted a mixture of legit fights and shoot-style pro wrestling. There Frank took on future training partner Tsuyoshi Kohsaka in a legit match.

Kohsaka had a thirty-pound weight advantage going into the fight with Shamrock, but just past the eleven-minute mark, Shamrock locked Kohsaka in a guillotine choke. Kohsaka was forced to use a rope break to get out of the hold, and when the fight went to the time limit, Kohsaka lost a point at the judges' table due to the rope break, so Shamrock won the decision.

The fight with Kohsaka was important, as soon after, Kohsaka went to train with Frank Shamrock and Maurice Smith. The Alliance, as they were known, came to be one of the most influential training camps in mixed martial arts history.

The reason The Alliance had such an impact on mixed martial arts is that the cross-training between Shamrock, Smith, and Kohsaka led Shamrock to improve in terms of kickboxing, making him a more complete, and thus more dominating, fighter once he entered the UFC Middleweight division soon after. Maurice Smith's career would not have been nearly so successful without Shamrock, as it was the groundfighting training they did together that led Smith to the Extreme Fighting Heavyweight title and, more importantly, the UFC Heavyweight title. When Smith defeated Mark Coleman for the UFC Heavyweight title, it was the first time a fighter with a primarily kickboxing background had defeated a fighter with a primarily wrestling background. Smith was able to defeat Coleman because of the cross-training in groundfighting and cardio work he had done with Frank Shamrock. "It just made it plain and a little more clear," says Shamrock about the continually developing technique of MMA and his part in it, "like the old saying that everything works, but nothing works for long. And that holds true to fighting."

Shamrock competed in another North American MMA fight after that, at the World Pankration Championships event in Texas on October 26, 1997. The event featured numerous other Lion's Den fighters, including Mikey Burnett, Vernon White, Tra Telligman, and Guy Mezger. There Shamrock defeated Wes Gassaway, who was disqualified due to rope escapes.

Frank returned to Japan for his next fight, a Shooto competition at the Japan Vale Tudo event on November 29, 1997. Shamrock took on the highly regarded (and tough) Enson Inoue, who outweighed him by a significant margin.

After a very close first round, Shamrock nailed Inoue with a hard knee, dropping him to the canvas. In a state of panic, Egan Inoue, Enson's brother, ran into the ring and shoved Shamrock away from Enson to prevent any more serious damage. Egan's interference in the bout led to a disqualification, and added another win to Shamrock's record.

The victory over Enson Inoue was an important step for Frank, as it had a twofold effect. First, it led Frank to compete in the UFC's first-ever event in Japan just a few weeks later, in which Frank made his UFC debut. Second, competing in UFC led Frank Shamrock and the Lion's Den to part ways in a not-so-amicable manner.

In early 1997, Ken Shamrock, who had operated the Lion's Den up to that point, signed a lucrative deal with the WWF to work full time as a professional wrestler. This meant that he would no longer have time to run the Lion's Den, and that someone would have to take it over. He left it in the hands of Frank and Jerry Bohlander, and Bob Shamrock managed the Lion's Den fighters' contracts with promotions such as the UFC.

Frank and Ken had a severe falling out over the way Frank was running the

Lion's Den, and a mere two weeks before his UFC debut at the Ultimate Japan event on December 21, 1997, Frank, who was still living with Bob Shamrock, took a pair of boxing gloves and left the Lion's Den for good.

At the UFC's Ultimate Japan event, just weeks after his departure from the Lion's Den, Frank came up against one of the top middleweight fighters in UFC, Kevin Jackson, in a match to determine the UFC's first Middleweight champion. A top-level amateur wrestler throughout the 1980s and the early '90s, Jackson had wrestled as a four-time NCAA All-American and captured a gold medal in freestyle wrestling in the 180.5-pound class at the '92 Olympics in Barcelona. He had scored a submission win over the man who defeated Frank Shamrock in SuperBrawl, John Lober, in Extreme Fighting, and had debuted in UFC at UFC 14, winning a four-man lightweight tournament by stopping Todd Butler in the first round and submitting Tony Fryklund in the finals. Jackson was undefeated in UFC.

Despite the fact that Kevin Jackson was no pushover opponent, Shamrock, in fact, pushed him over in a figurative sense, shocking the world as he submitted Jackson in just sixteen seconds with an armbar to win the UFC Middleweight title. This win, because it showed what Frank could do in the UFC and also because it happened just shortly after Frank left the Lion's Den, helped Frank step out of Ken's shadow in mixed martial arts and establish a legacy of his own in the UFC.

The win was monumental because it started Frank on a five-fight winning streak in the UFC, cementing his reputation as one of the greatest fighters to ever step into the octagon. Shamrock becoming the first Middleweight champion (the title was known sometimes as the Lightweight title and also as the Middleweight title during that period in UFC) was also important, because his early success in defending the Middleweight title as an event headliner established the current UFC Light-Heavyweight title (which the Middleweight title would evolve into) as the most sought-after and popular championships for UFC fighters and fans alike. Nearly every major box-office-drawing-card fighter in the UFC today has competed for the Light-Heavyweight belt at one point or another, including Tito Ortiz, Wanderlei Silva, Randy Couture, Vitor Belfort, Chuck Liddell, and even Ken Shamrock, among many others.

Frank defended his newly won title for the first time on March 13, 1998, at UFC 16. His opponent was Igor Zinoviev, who had won a four-man tournament in Extreme Fighting a few years earlier. A veteran of that organization, Zinoviev had also fought to a draw against John Lober at Extreme Fighting 3, and was undefeated going into the fight against Shamrock.

Well, that changed in only twenty-two seconds—just the time it took Shamrock to knock Zinoviev out with a huge highlight reel–style slam, a slam that effectively ended Zinoviev's MMA career. From that slam alone, Zinoviev suffered a broken collarbone, a fractured vertebra, and a dislocated shoulder.

After visiting Zinoviev in the hospital, Shamrock got over any feelings of remorse he may have had about the fight, as there wasn't much time between this fight and the next. Shamrock was approached by the UFC to fight on the very next show on May 15, 1998, in a bout that would not be broadcast on pay-per-view. Fabiano Iha was originally selected as Shamrock's opponent, but he was deemed too small, so they came up with another name: Jeremy Horn. Horn was a little-known independent fighter at the time, who had been building up a reputation in Iowa as an excellent competitor, having taken much larger Dan Severn to a draw.

Shamrock went into the fight with a shoulder injury and very little training. Horn was able to take Shamrock down right away, proving himself to be a great fighter by regularly going for submissions and looking to finish the fight. Horn dominated the entire regulation period of the fight, and made Shamrock look out of place, as though he was the one making his debut in UFC, not the other way around.

Nevertheless, Shamrock's resilience shone through in this fight as, when the opportunity arose a few minutes into the first overtime period, Shamrock caught Horn in a kneebar and tapped his opponent out. It was very close for Shamrock, but he emerged the victor. That was the last time that Shamrock went into a fight unprepared.

Shamrock's next bout, his fourth in the UFC, brought him a chance to avenge an old loss; he took on John Lober, headlining UFC's Ultimate Brazil in Sao Paulo on October 16, 1998. Since losing their initial fight via split-decision back in SuperBrawl, Shamrock had defeated Igor Zinoviev, who had gone to a draw with Lober, and Kevin Jackson, who had submitted Lober in Extreme Fighting. It was time for Shamrock to correct his only loss since leaving Pancrase.

Lober's game plan was to get inside of Shamrock's head and psych him out by acting as obnoxious as possible.

Lober was clearly successful in getting inside Shamrock's head, although he should have been careful about what he wished for, as Shamrock went into that fight with an unprecedented vengeance. To show how much Shamrock wanted to punish Lober in that fight, early in the bout Shamrock had even locked him in a guillotine choke, but he let go because he wanted to continue to serve him with damage.

Lober took such a beating that he submitted at just under eight minutes, giving Shamrock the win. He later approached Shamrock to apologize for his behavior prior to the fight, explaining that it was all part of a strategy that ended up backfiring.

It appeared this would be Shamrock's last UFC match, as his contract with SEG, UFC's parent company, had expired. His relationship with SEG had always been strained, and Shamrock decided to step down while he was still the UFC Middleweight champion.

Meanwhile, a young, brash fighter by the name of Tito Ortiz was rising up very quickly through the UFC ranks, having defeated two Lion's Den fighters, Jerry Bohlander and Guy Mezger, in very convincing manner. After fighting Mezger, Ortiz even nearly got into a post-fight confrontation with Ken

Shamrock, who was cornering Mezger. It was becoming very clear that Ortiz was on a different level than the other fighters in UFC at that time.

Shamrock saw this, and the challenge to him was to come back for one more fight and see if he could beat the fighter who was dominating the Middleweight division of UFC.

Shamrock was the underdog going into the fight, which took place at UFC 22 on September 24, 1999. Despite the fact that Ortiz and Shamrock both competed as middleweights, Ortiz had a considerable weight advantage over Frank going into the fight, and knew how to use his weight to his full advantage. "I couldn't submit Tito—he was way too strong," says Frank. "I couldn't knock him out, and I tried to do that. He was just too big."

The fight changed the meaning of cardio conditioning for MMA fighters. To defeat Ortiz, Shamrock had to outlast him. It was a war of attrition. Shamrock had trained his heart out for the fight, and he was just going to have to make Tito bring the fight to him. Despite how skilled a fighter may be, he can't do much, if anything, if he is out of gas.

With Maurice Smith in his corner, Shamrock took punishment during the first three rounds of the bout, as Tito used his size and weight advantage and his wrestling skills to damage Frank. In the fourth round, though, the tides started to turn, as the amount of punishment Tito had dished out in the first three rounds caught up with him, and he began to tire. Shamrock managed to control the bout on the ground, and, with just seconds left on the clock, he rose to his feet. Tito didn't follow him up, and Shamrock dropped a devastating elbow down onto Ortiz to end the fight, pulling a come-from-behind victory out of his bag by stopping Tito Ortiz in the fourth round of a fight that Shamrock would most likely have lost if it had gone to the judges' cards. Shamrock didn't come out of the fight unmarked, though; he'd fractured his right hand, took thirteen stitches in his head, and cracked his anklebone. It was the most memorable fight from that era of UFC. Tito Ortiz learned from this loss, as he followed Frank Shamrock's example and turned himself into a cardio machine, ensuring that he would never again lose a fight due to lack of conditioning.

"[Frank Shamrock's] cardio conditioning was outstanding, and many fighters learned that what they thought was 'in shape' was not," writes John McCarthy, who refereed the bout between Shamrock and Ortiz, in an e-mail to the author. "Tito Ortiz is a perfect example of a fighter that learned about conditioning from Frank. Tito is a much better fighter now because of his approach to the fight and his preparation. He learned it from Frank."

After the fight, Shamrock opted to retire. Although his win over Ortiz was definitely his final bout in UFC, Shamrock's overall retirement from MMA lasted just over a year, until he signed a deal with K-1 in Japan to go up against Australian fighter Elvis Sinosic at the 2000 K-1 Grand Prix Finals on December 10, 2000. Although K-1 fights were generally kickboxing bouts, this fight was held under MMA rules.

Shamrock went into the fight against Sinosic with a severed tendon in his right shoulder. Despite the injury, Shamrock also went into the fight with a striker's mentality and tried for a standup battle against Sinosic. Although he ended up winning a decision, the fight was a somewhat disappointing return to competition for Shamrock, as he wasn't able to finish Sinosic during the body of the fight. "I look at every fight as a war, and someone has to win the war, or the war should just keep going on," says Shamrock.

Always looking to improve himself as a fighter, Shamrock signed on for yet another new challenge, fighting Shannon Ritch at a K-1 show in Las Vegas under K-1 kickboxing rules on August 11, 2001. In preparation, Shamrock underwent detailed training in kickboxing, and this had a real impact: Shamrock broke Ritch's arm with a roundhouse kick merely fifty-six seconds in, ending the fight.

Not only does Shamrock constantly seek to improve his skills as a fighter, but he also understands what makes people buy tickets and pay-per-views for these mixed martial arts events, and he tries to focus on that as well. "In reality, people are there for the story—the fight is how the story plays out," he says. "I know what's missing from our sport, and I have just taken steps to add that final piece of the story for the fans. Fighting is fighting, and kickboxing, boxing, and wrestling are all the same thing—it's the story that everyone follows. I want to create stories."

During his brief K-1 run and afterwards, Shamrock was also acting in film, television, and commercials in addition to training other fighters, and he later promoted a number of MMA events. Rumors have circulated for years about Shamrock coming into PRIDE to compete against the biggest star in Japan, Kazushi Sakuraba. The fight with Sakuraba never occurred, because Shamrock and PRIDE weren't able to work out a contract to get the two men in the same ring at the same time.

Shamrock took a couple of years off from actual competition, and returned at a WEC event in California titled "Return of a Legend" on March 27, 2003, to defeat the much larger Bryan Pardoe via submission to win the WEC Light-Heavyweight title.

The question of how Frank would fare in MMA now that he's so far removed from competing against other top-tier MMA fighters is a question that has yet to be answered. "[Frank] made his own name; he really didn't make his name off of Ken," says MMA promoter and former UFC commentator Jeff Osborne in a phone interview with the author of this book. "He hasn't fought [in UFC] since 1999, and he's still unproven in today's game in lots of people's minds."

"[Frank] was one of the first truly versatile fighters in the UFC who also defeated top competition," writes Stephen Quadros in an e-mail to the author. "It could be argued that he was America's first fully realized mixed martial artist on a technical level."

"I never did it to be a star. I just did it to be really good at something," says Shamrock.

Mixed martial arts competition was redefined by Frank Shamrock when he bridged the early days of the UFC, featuring karate masters, sumos, and jeet kune do experts, to the modern era of UFC action, featuring many of the most complete fighters on Earth. Fighters are now fully aware of the extreme importance of cardio conditioning, pre-fight strategy, and combining standup striking skills with grappling skills on the ground. They are fully aware in part because of Frank Shamrock.

Ken Shamrock

The North American mainstream recognizes him more than any other mixed martial artist who has competed on the continent. Anybody who has ever watched an MMA event or a pro wrestling show knows who he is. For years, he has represented the ideal look, talk, and charisma for a headline fighter in North America. Nicknamed "The World's Most Dangerous Man," he's a former UFC Superfight champion, and ranks alongside Royce Gracie as the biggest box-office draw in UFC history. His name is Ken Shamrock.

The youngest of three brothers, Shamrock was born Kenneth Wayne Kilpatrick on February 11, 1964, in Macon, Georgia, to Richard and Diane Kilpatrick. Richard and Diane ended up divorcing, leaving Diane to take care of Ken and his brothers, Ritchie and Robbie. When Ken was five, his mother remarried, this time to an army aviator named Bob Nance, and they all moved to Napa, California.

Shamrock had a rough upbringing. As a child, he often got into fights and was no stranger to the police. He ran away from home for the first time at the age of ten. He stayed in an abandoned car with a group of other runaways until an older boy stabbed him and he wound up in the hospital. He eventually found himself in the care of Bob Shamrock and his group home.

Having raised more than 600 boys at his ranch, the Shamrock Ranch for Boys, Bob Shamrock had developed a reputation for being very good at dealing with troubled young men. This ranch is where Ken spent the rest of his youth. He grew close to Bob, who eventually legally adopted Ken, giving the boy his last name. Later, when Ken was in mixed martial arts and pro wrestling, Bob Shamrock also worked with Ken as his manager.

Bob Shamrock regularly staged boxing matches between feuding kids at the Shamrock Ranch, aiming to quell disorderly conduct through organized sport. Although Ken excelled in these little bouts, as a teenager he also continued to get into numerous street fights. Recognizing Ken's natural athletic ability, Bob Shamrock decided to enroll him in high-school sports, including football and wrestling.

Ken excelled in wrestling, but in his senior high-school year, he suffered a serious neck injury; his opponent had hoisted him onto his shoulders for a suplex but slipped, and avalanched down onto Shamrock. Ken suffered two fractured vertebrae, and had to have a metal halo screwed into his skull to keep his spine from shifting. His doctors told him that he would never be able to participate in contact sports again. Of course, Ken would later prove those doctors to be very wrong.

After high-school, Ken competed regularly in street fights for cash. He competed in his first Toughman bout at the age of nineteen. He excelled in this, and subsequently won multiple tournaments. In 1988, when Ken wasn't doing much other than bouncing at nightclubs and fighting in Toughman bouts, he entered into the unique world of professional wrestling upon a suggestion from Bob Shamrock.

Shamrock first trained briefly under Buzz Sawyer in Sacramento before relocating to North Carolina to train under Nelson Royal and Gene Anderson. After training under Royal and Anderson for a number of months, Shamrock began to work dates at small independent wrestling shows in North Carolina and elsewhere, first under the name of Wayne Shamrock (a name he also used later in Japan, during his days in Pancrase), and then under the name of "Mr. Wrestling" Vince Torrelli. These shows generally drew crowds of fewer than 100 fans, and small promotions frequently opened and closed without anyone taking notice. Although Shamrock, not having been a fan of professional wrestling as a child (as many other pro wrestlers were), had gotten into the business mainly to make money, he would have been making such small payoffs on the independent level that it would likely cost more in gas to drive to the event than he was getting paid to wrestle.

Shamrock eventually met and worked with respected undercard wrestler Dean Malenko, who introduced him to the shoot style of pro wrestling that a company called UWF was promoting in Japan. Whereas North American pro wrestling is heavily gimmicked, with colorful personas, costumes, and entrances—and is clearly less than real—shoot-style pro wrestling in Japan, like UWF, was promoted to look very real, the wrestlers were very stiff with each other in the matches, and at some points only the trained eye could tell the difference between a shoot-style pro wrestling match and a legitimate bout.

Malenko introduced Shamrock to a foreign talent agent for the UWF, Masami Soranaka, and under the name Wayne Shamrock, Ken soon made his debut with the company.

"Sammy Soranaka was the first one that introduced them to [submission wrestling] in Tampa, Florida," recalls Shamrock in an interview conducted for this book. "He introduced me to the submission game."

UWF and Shamrock were a natural fit. Since UWF promoted a realistic style, Shamrock was taught the finer points of legitimate submission wrestling to improve the quality of his pro wrestling bouts.

In the late 1980s in Japan, the UWF was incredibly popular, but the promotion soon splintered apart into separate companies. Shamrock had started with UWF during its last few months, and ended up leaving the company in the midst of the turmoil to join one of the start-up companies, Pro Wrestling Fujiwara Gumi (PWFG), promoted by Yoshiaki Fujiwara. Shamrock had found quick success working initially in UWF and then in PWFG, and had become one of the five or so most popular foreign wrestling stars in Japan at the time.

Fujiwara was a pro wrestler who had learned submission wrestling from notorious pro wrestling tough guy and shootfighter Karl Gotch, a foreigner who worked regularly in Japan for many years. Gotch had become legendary in Japan as a mean, legitimate bad man and tough guy, having taught an entire crew of popular Japanese pro wrestlers the art of submission wrestling.

Shamrock wasn't in the PWFG long before a split in that company occurred, and talented undercard wrestlers Masakatsu Funaki and Minoru Suzuki, tired of being held down in the card by aging owner Fujiwara, left PWFG to form what would become one of the most legendary promotions in the history of the business and the final step in a decades-long evolution of pro wrestling in Japan: Pancrase. Shamrock went with them.

Pancrase was the very first professional wrestling promotion to promote nearly 100 percent real fights, holding their first event on September 21, 1993, less than two months before the UFC's debut over in the United States. Pancrase changed the business forever, and Ken Shamrock, at the forefront of Pancrase as one of their top three stars (along with Suzuki and Funaki), was a major part of this revolution.

Before Pancrase formed, Shamrock had already been tested as a fighter in PWFG. When they had booked him in a real fight on October 4, 1992, at the Tokyo Dome against legendary kickboxer Don Nakaya Nielsen, Shamrock defeated Nielsen in just forty-five seconds, taking the kickboxer down right away. As a kickboxer, Nielsen had no training in groundfighting, and was quickly caught in a leg submission by Shamrock. Shamrock had proven in the PWFG that he had what it takes in a real fight, and he would get the chance to prove this again in Pancrase.

When Pancrase held their first show, the term "mixed martial arts" didn't even exist. It was just "real pro wrestling," and the fan base for Pancrase was composed completely of Japanese pro wrestling fans. Pancrase was seen as a pro wrestling group because it was the first company to build itself around pro wrestlers doing legitimate fights, and the rules of the fights were taken right out of pro wrestling. Just like in pro wrestling, in Pancrase you couldn't hit the head or face with a closed first, and you had to let go of your submission hold if your opponent reached the ropes.

At the time, no one knew what to expect. Pancrase sold out NK Hall in Tokyo to 7,000 fans for their debut show. Shamrock, Funaki, and Suzuki all showed up looking in great shape. Suzuki blew through his opponent in the opening fight of the night, and in the main event, Shamrock and Funaki squared off against one another. Shamrock was able to take Funaki down in the early part of the fight, and dominated the ground game until the fighters reached a stalemate and were restarted on their feet. Again, Shamrock managed to get Funaki on the mat, and finished him with a side choke. The show set the stage for the mixed martial arts revolution that would later hit Japan with companies like RINGS and, more importantly, PRIDE, as Pancrase got pro wrestling fans in Japan to tune in to MMA promotions rather than traditional-style pro wrestling promotions.

Pancrase held their second show on October 14, 1993, at the Tsuyuhashi Sports Center, where Shamrock took on Yoshiki Takahashi. Takahashi was able to take Shamrock down multiple times during the fight, but Shamrock was able to nearly catch Takahashi in a side choke at different points, and also nailed him in the face with a hard palm strike before heel hooking him for the submission victory. The heel hook was an extremely dangerous move at the time because many of the fighters' knowledge of submissions was primitive, and they didn't know how to block such a technique. More than a couple of wrestlers ended up in hospital because of heel hooking, and the move was banned. Shamrock would later become known as a master of that technique.

Over in the United States, Rorion Gracie and Art Davie, along with the pay-per-view company Semaphore Entertainment Group, had put together the idea of a one-night, eight-man, style versus style promotion that would take place on pay-per-view. It was to be called the Ultimate Fighting

Championship. Shamrock heard of the promotion, called Art Davie about participating in the first tournament, and sent in an application. Davie ended up selecting Shamrock to be one of the first fighters to ever compete in the UFC. In the UFC, Shamrock would fight under the name Ken Shamrock, instead of under the ring name, Wayne Shamrock, that he'd used in Japan.

The first UFC event took place on November 12, 1993, in Denver. Unsure of whether the UFC would actually happen or not, or even what the deal with the promotion was, Shamrock competed in one last fight in Pancrase on November 8, and defeated Takaku Fuke via submission in under a minute before taking the long flight from Japan back to the United States.

When he arrived in Colorado for the debut UFC event, his chiseled musculature and superstar good looks, combined with his experience in Pancrase and street fighting, made him an instant favorite amongst those in attendance, leading to predictions that he'd take the entire tournament.

His first-round opponent was hometown favorite Patrick Smith, whose background was in kickboxing. Much like he'd done in his win over Don Nakaya Nielsen, Shamrock took Smith down and heel hooked him for the submission victory in less than two minutes. Although the crowd booed the loss of their hometown favorite, Shamrock had been impressive in his first UFC fight, and proceeded to move on into the second round of the tournament.

It was at this point that his legendary feud with Royce Gracie began. One of many sons of Helio Gracie, the creator of Brazilian Jiu Jitsu, Royce heralded from that sport's largest and most respected fighting family. But going into the second round of this tournament, he was many pounds lighter than the huge Shamrock, and anyone looking at the two would think that, simply because of the size difference, Shamrock would easily walk through Royce en route to the finals.

But that isn't what happened. At the start of the fight, they immediately went to the ground, where Shamrock went for an ankle lock. Royce managed to avoid the hold, though, and once the opportunity arose, he sunk in a rear naked choke. Shamrock tapped out, but the referee didn't see it at first and didn't stop the fight. Royce quickly complained to the ref, and Shamrock admitted that he had indeed tapped. It was over in fifty-seven seconds, and just as quickly, a feud was born. In Japan, Pancrase didn't emphasize the use of chokes in their fights because they weren't as exciting as other moves, such as heel hooks or armbars, so Shamrock had little experience to draw on in defending Royce's choke in this fight. Shamrock also didn't know how to defend against the gi, which Royce wore and used as a weapon in the match.

Although Shamrock didn't make it to the finals of the first UFC tournament, his star would rise in UFC upon his return to the octagon to seek revenge against Royce nearly a year later.

In the meantime, Shamrock continued as one of the top stars and the top foreign box-office drawing card in Pancrase. He returned to Pancrase with a victory by quickly submitting Andre Van Den Oetelaar in just over a minute on December 8, 1993. From there, Shamrock suffered his first loss in Pancrase, ending his four-fight undefeated streak in that promotion by losing to Minoru Suzuki on January 19, 1994, when Suzuki submitted him in just over seven minutes in the main event of the card. This loss was one of only two legitimate losses Shamrock ever suffered during his entire run in Pancrase, which spanned over two years and eighteen legitimate fights. Shamrock bounced back from that loss with a submission victory over Ryushi Yanagisawa on April 21, 1994.

Even though fights in Pancrase are generally considered under the umbrella of mixed martial arts, Shamrock did compete in one kickboxing rules fight at a Pancrase show on May 31, 1994, against Frank "The Animal" Lobman, a kickboxer from the Netherlands. Lobman chopped Shamrock down with leg kicks, and finally managed to knock Shamrock out with a kick at 5:25. Shamrock lost the bout, but because it was under kickboxing rules, which didn't allow for groundfighting, and because Shamrock was known as a submissions fighter at the time, the loss did little, if any, damage to his image in Japan.

Although Pancrase was built on the foundation of presenting legitimate fights, there were a few worked matches here and there. Top fighters such as Suzuki, Shamrock, and Masakatsu Funaki were known for carrying lesser fighters to longer and more exciting bouts in Pancrase in order to give ticket-buying fans their money's worth, rather than icing off their opponents in quick fashion (which, for the most part, they could have done).

Shamrock was involved in at least two possible works in Pancrase, the first against Matt Hume on July 6, 1994, in which Shamrock defeated Hume via submission at 5:50. The reason why the Shamrock-Hume fight may have been worked is not exactly known.

"I think one of the two was injured," says Dave Meltzer, editor of the *Wrestling Observer*, which covers both pro wrestling and mixed martial arts. "Since Ken won, I'm guessing Matt asked for it because he was hurt." Hume fought again in Pancrase just twenty days later, losing via submission to Manabu Yamada, so it's hard to say whether or not Hume was injured, or what the case was with this match.

After the match against Matt Hume, Shamrock came back with a win, this time submitting Dutch kickboxing master Bas Rutten on July 26, 1994. Bas had yet to master the ground game of MMA at that point in his career, and Shamrock was able to submit him just past the sixteen-minute mark in the bout. It would be the first of two victories Shamrock would achieve over Bas in Pancrase.

On September 1, 1994, Shamrock suffered his second and final legitimate loss in Pancrase, this time to top superstar Masakatsu Funaki just eight days before Shamrock returned to fight at UFC 3 in another eight-man tournament. In the main event of the card, held at the Osaka Metropolitan Gym, Funaki was able to submit Shamrock in just 2:30. Shamrock would have the opportunity to avenge this loss in Pancrase a little over a year later.

In the meantime, Shamrock went back to the U.S. to seek his revenge against Royce Gracie at UFC 3. Buyrates had continued to climb for the UFC, and UFC 3, advertised around the idea of Shamrock and Royce meeting in the tournament finals, proved to be the catalyst that sent UFC to set the kind of pay-per-view buyrate records that still stand to this day.

Shamrock and Royce clearly disliked each other. Royce felt that Shamrock would not confess to being submitted by him in the first UFC tournament, and Shamrock, upset about his loss to the smaller man, wanted to prove something to himself by getting Royce back into the octagon. In the first round of the tournament, Shamrock defeated judoka Christophe Leninger in just under five minutes, and went on to choke out Felix Lee Mitchell in just under five minutes in the second round, sending himself to the tournament finals.

The problem for Ken was that Royce Gracie had been rocked in a full-throttle, exciting fight with newcomer Kimo Leopoldo in the first round, and was so exhausted that, when he came out for his second-round bout against Harold Howard, Royce had his corner throw in the towel before the fight could actually take place. This eliminated Shamrock's chance to get back at Royce in the finals of the UFC 3 tournament.

Shamrock had not returned to the UFC for the fame or the money, but rather to seek revenge against the small Brazilian man who had defeated him in their first fight. Unable to exact that revenge at UFC 3, Shamrock claimed an ankle injury from his second-round fight with Mitchell and pulled out of the tournament. Steve Jennum took his place in the finals and defeated Harold Howard to win the UFC 3 tournament. Shamrock's aura in the United States really started to grow after this event, because, despite the fact that he hadn't won the tournament, he also hadn't lost a fight in UFC since losing to Royce (casual UFC fans in the United States would not have been aware of Shamrock's losses in Pancrase in Japan), and he had made it clear that he wanted to get Royce back in the octagon. It was turning into a fight that a lot of fans were willing to pay a lot of money to see.

Shamrock returned to Pancrase in Japan, taking on and defeating Takaku

Fuke for the second time in his career on October 15, 1994, as he submitted Fuke with a rear naked choke at 3:13.

Following that fight was the biggest tournament in Pancrase history, and one of the more important tournaments in mixed martial arts at that point in time: the King of Pancrase championship tournament, held in December 1994. The two-day, sixteen-man tournament for the King of Pancrase title belt would take place at Sumo Hall on December 16 and 17, featuring all of the top fighters Pancrase had to offer, including Ken, Frank Shamrock, Bas Rutten, Maurice Smith, Matt Hume, Masakatsu Funaki, Minoru Suzuki, Jason DeLucia, Manabu Yamada, Vernon White, Takaku Fuke, and others.

In the first night of action, before a sell-out crowd of 11,000 fans, Shamrock defeated Alex Cook via submission at 1:31 in the first round of the tournament, and was sent into the second round to take on future training partner Maurice Smith, who had knocked out Takaku Fuke in less than three minutes in his first-round bout. Smith, nearly a pure kickboxer at that time and not overly familiar with submissions or submissions defense, was tapped out by Shamrock at 4:23 of their fight, putting Shamrock in the third round of the tournament, taking place the following night.

The second night of action at Sumo Hall also sold out, as 11,000 fans came to see Shamrock take on Masakatsu Funaki in the third round in a rematch of the very first main event in Pancrase history. Funaki had submitted both Todd Bjornethun and Vernon White to make it to this point in the tournament. Shamrock was able to submit Funaki at 5:50 of the fight, but the bout nearly cost him dearly, as he blew out his knee while fighting Funaki. He didn't want to come out for the finals because of the injury, but he was talked into going out and doing it, which resulted in a long and boring final round with Manabu Yamada, who had submitted Christopher DeWeaver and Frank Shamrock in the first night and had submitted Minoru Suzuki with an armbar earlier in the second night to make it this far. Shamrock simply out-wrestled Yamada for thirty minutes and won a judges' decision.

It was significant that Shamrock became the first King of Pancrase, because it was the first time in at least seventy-five years that a pro wrestling promotion had a major male world champion who had won the title in a legitimate (not worked) fight. It had been so long since a pro wrestling title such as this had been regularly defended in legitimate fights that no one in the industry would have been around to see the last time it had happened. It was truly one of the most monumental tournaments and title wins in history.

Shamrock continued to fight in Pancrase after this, defending the title on January 26, 1995, against Leon Dijk, whom he defeated via submission at 4:45. He followed that up with the second victory of his career over Bas Rutten, when he quickly submitted Bas with a kneebar just a little over one minute into the fight on March 10, 1995. That fight went down as the final loss of Rutten's career, as he would go undefeated from that point on in twenty-one straight fights.

Shamrock went on to take part in the most important fight of his career up to that point, returning to the UFC to finally get his revenge against Royce Gracie at UFC 5 on April 7, 1995, in Charlotte, North Carolina. UFC 5 was the most-watched UFC event in history up to that point in time, mainly because fans would finally get to see Ken Shamrock step back into the octagon to take on Royce. Royce had remained undefeated in UFC, and the only tournament he lost was due to the fact that he couldn't continue due to exhaustion at UFC 3, so in the fans' eyes, he was the rightful winner of each UFC tournament. Royce had shown few, if any, flaws in the UFC up to this point, but the feeling was that if anyone could defeat Royce, it would be Ken Shamrock. To make the fight even more interesting, SEG, the parent company of UFC, came up with the idea of the Superfight title to be awarded to the winner of the bout. The Superfight title would eventually become the UFC Heavyweight title that is defended today.

The show drew a 1.05 buyrate and over 260,000 buys on pay-per-view, and remains to this day the second most-watched UFC pay-per-view of all time, right behind their very next event, UFC 6, which was headlined by Ken Shamrock versus Dan Severn.

Unfortunately for UFC fans across the globe, Shamrock versus Gracie II didn't live up to the pre-fight hype, as both men went out there and fought to a very long thirty-six-minute draw. Most of the fight saw Shamrock on the ground in Royce's guard, and Shamrock, not adept with working within the guard or against an opponent with a gi, wasn't willing to commit to doing anything because he didn't want to make a mistake.

"The first time [I fought Royce] I got caught off guard, and the second I went in there and basically eliminated all of his offense," said Shamrock. "And they put the time limit on prior to that event. I wanted to wear him out and show that I was in better shape than him, and show that my skill level was above his. I trained for a two-hour fight, and I was working for a two-hour fight. When they changed the time limit, I couldn't really change my strategy, since it was something I was working on for a while."

Royce wasn't willing to commit to a mistake in the fight either, so they spent most of the fight just lying there. Late in the fight, however, Shamrock was able to punch Royce in the face while they were on their feet, bloodying Royce and raising a mouse under his eye. "That right hand in overtime hurt [Royce]. That was the first time he'd ever been really hit. It was a big eye-opener for him," says Shamrock. "He's never really been hit hard where he's been busted open."

The fight ended in a draw, but most people watching the fight feel that, if UFC at the time had had ringside judges, Shamrock would have easily won the decision. But there were no ringside judges, and Shamrock had to settle for the moral victory rather than the real one. The Superfight title remained vacant. "It wasn't a victory by any means, because I would've liked to have finished him, but I ran out of time," says Shamrock. "I would've won a unanimous decision [had there been judges], but I wanted to finish him. I believe if I was able to fight him with the rules that were set down . . . that was the first time ever UFC put in a time limit, and it just so happened they put it in when I fought Royce Gracie. And without that time limit, I'd beat him."

Shamrock had proven that he was on Royce's level as a fighter by not losing to him and by leaving him bloodied, but before they could meet in the octagon again, Royce chose to depart the UFC for good. Shamrock remained, taking Gracie's position as UFC's biggest name and box-office drawing card. He continued to headline for UFC regularly from this point forward while still fighting for Pancrase in Japan.

Problems arose between Shamrock and Pancrase at this point, however. Dan Severn had won the eight-man UFC 5 tournament, and SEG had decided to book Severn against Ken Shamrock in the main event of UFC 6 for the vacant UFC Superfight title. At the time, Severn was also working as a pro wrestler on the independent level, and because of his fame from the UFC, the National Wrestling Alliance—which had been the most powerful pro wrestling organization worldwide for decades but had since crumbled down to nothing but a network of independent promotions—decided to put the NWA World title on him, hoping to bring exposure back to their organization.

So, at the time of the proposed Severn versus Shamrock fight, Severn was also the world champion of a "fake" pro wrestling organization. Pancrase hated the idea that its world champion, Shamrock, who had won the title and defended it in legitimate fights, would seriously risk losing to a fake pro-wrestling world champion. That would undermine everything that Pancrase stood for. Furthermore, Severn had also worked as an undercard pro wrestler in Japan years earlier, and didn't approach Shamrock's level of popularity in that country.

Pancrase asked Shamrock to drop the King of Pancrase title in a worked fight to Minoru Suzuki on May 13, 1995 (about two months before he fought Severn at UFC 6), at Tokyo Bay NK Hall, and because he was making far more money in UFC than he was in Pancrase, Shamrock agreed to it. He lost the match against Suzuki, tapping out to a kneebar just over two minutes into the fixed bout. The irony that Pancrase had Shamrock drop their title in a fake match within their own organization so he wouldn't fight someone who held a "fake" pro wrestling championship was obviously lost on the promotion.

Shamrock's relationship with Pancrase continued to disintegrate, and he only competed in three more fights for the organization, all within months after his worked loss to Suzuki. He fought in the opening match of Pancrase's card at Korakuen Hall on July 22, 1995, submitting Larry Papadopoulos with an Achilles lock in 2:18. He returned to Pancrase on December 14, 1995, quickly submitting Katsuomi Inagaki. His final bout with Pancrase was on January 28, 1996, at the Yokohama Culture Gym, where he won a decision over Yoshiki Takahashi. After that fight, Shamrock never fought for Pancrase again.

Pancrase had been operating as a successful pro wrestling promotion using real fighters in legitimate fights rather than worked bouts, and was the first promotion ever to do so. They set historical milestones and records in the business, but by early 1996, Pancrase's future was not as bright as it appeared. They had overspent on their top talent. Another one of the main problems with Pancrase was that, although the vast majority of their matches were legitimate, they kept a full schedule similar to a worked pro wrestling company, which burnt out most of their regulars and all of their stars because the schedule was just too packed to do real fights. Masakatsu Funaki and Minoru Suzuki, due to a combination of burnout, accumulating injuries, age, and the overall advancement of techniques used in mixed martial arts, were only shells of the fighters they used to be. Bas Rutten left for UFC and then retired. Frank Shamrock left for UFC and then retired. Guy Mezger left for UFC and then PRIDE. Maurice Smith left for Extreme Fighting, where he became a bigger star than he ever would have been in Pancrase; then he moved to UFC. Yuki Kondo and Yoshiki Takahashi didn't have the name value to carry the promotion into the next era, and Pancrase was unable to develop any new stars to sustain the promotion when the original stars faded away.

Contract problems cropped up between Pancrase and Shamrock. Ken had a big-money contract with Pancrase, but was making more with the UFC, which had become a huge hit on pay-per-view at that time, and there were conflicts over dates that Shamrock didn't want to work but Pancrase wanted to book him on. There was a big blow-up between the two parties, and Shamrock ended up walking out of the promotion in '96.

"I think Pancrase was running low on money, and Ken had a big contract, and they wanted to create a problem to save face," Dave Meltzer suggests. "You can see after that point they stopped using big names, for the most part."

As retaliation for Ken's quitting, Pancrase fired Frank Juarez Shamrock, Ken's adopted brother who also grew up at the Shamrock Ranch, even though Frank had absolutely nothing to do with any of the problems between Ken and Pancrase.

Frank, at that point in time, was a part of the Lion's Den fighting team that Shamrock had formed, which at times also included Guy Mezger, Jerry Bohlander, Mikey Burnett, and Pete Williams. Maurice Smith also trained regularly with Ken before he began to work predominantly with Frank Shamrock and Tsuyoshi Kohsaka later on.

The formation of the Lion's Den was a very important part of mixed martial arts history, because this school set the standard for what fighters do by teaming them together to train and help each other improve. It was the first team of its kind in MMA.

"It was huge, because most people came in and trained with a few people, and they did this and they did that, but when I had the Lion's Den, there's still no group out there that have the same training philosophies and the same training schedules that the early Lion's Den had," says Shamrock regarding the influence of the Lion's Den on how fighters train today. "I mean, they lived in a fighter's house, which I took care of, and ate food that I took care of. I took care of these guys, but they trained from morning time to evening time, Monday through Friday, and then they had the weekend off. This was a school; this was a boot camp. They didn't quit, they kept going until they had their first pro fight, and if they wanted to leave after their first pro fight they could go out on their own. Most of the time they stayed. That was the regimen we had. These guys trained with each other, they lived with each other, they ate with each other, so these guys became very close, and they became very good. They'd go in with six months of training and beat guys who had been doing jiu jitsu for ten years."

The Lion's Den was originally opened in a warehouse in Lodi, California, and was far less than glamorous. The school's prime had passed after Ken Shamrock signed with the WWF in early 1997 and subsequently left the MMA world for a few years. Without its leader, the Lion's Den slowly dwindled down and became more of a legacy of MMA past than anything else.

Pancrase may have lost Shamrock in 1996, but he still had a ways to go in UFC. On July 14, 1995, in Casper, Wyoming, the most-watched UFC pay-per-view of all time took place. UFC 6 was headlined by Ken Shamrock versus Dan Severn, drawing a record buyrate of 1.1 for the promotion and over 260,000 buys on pay-per-view due to the power of the Severn-Shamrock confrontation.

Tensions between Severn and Shamrock were high by this point, and fans could see it. Shamrock had gone to his time-limit draw with Royce Gracie at UFC 5 in a fight that most people felt he had unofficially won, and meanwhile Severn had won the UFC 5 eight-man tournament in dominating fashion after losing to Gracie in the finals of the UFC 4 tournament. In a pre-fight press conference for UFC 6, Shamrock had made his feelings about the soft-spoken Severn very clear when Severn got up and left the press conference while Shamrock was being interviewed by the reporters, and suffice to say, neither man had many good things to say about the other—a fact that remains true even to this very day.

"When me and Dan fought in the first Superfight and I choked him out, prior to that we were doing an interview with Oleg Taktarov, myself, and

Severn," says Shamrock on the origins of his heat with Dan Severn. "And I remember all the questions were being directed towards me when we were in this room, and the interviewers were asking me a lot of questions. Severn got pissed off, got up, and walked out. I told Phyllis [Lee, Severn's manager] that was rude and that it pissed me off, and I said that I was just gonna beat him, but now I'm gonna hurt him. Phyllis said 'in your dreams,' and I said that we'll see about that. And I said I'm gonna hurt him bad."

The UFC Superfight championship title was on the line. Going into the fight, because of his weight advantage, his top-notch wrestling ability, and generally being perceived as an overall better fighter, Severn was the favorite to defeat Shamrock. What ended up happening was very different. Just 2:14 into the fight, Shamrock was able to make Severn tap out to a guillotine choke after Severn left his head open when he went for a takedown. It was over that quickly, and Shamrock had upset Severn and become the very first UFC Superfight champion.

During this time in UFC, Shamrock earned the nickname of "The World's Most Dangerous Man." "I got that while I was fighting in the UFC," said Shamrock in an interview with Pride FC. "It was a CNN special, The World's Most Dangerous Things. At first, I wasn't sure about it because the UFC was going through a lot of problems so I called them and asked them what they wanted to do. I thought they were going to put me in a bad way and do bad special but they really made me look good. They showed me with my kids and my family. It was good."

Shamrock returned to defend the Superfight title at UFC 7 on September 8, 1995, in Buffalo, New York, against Oleg Taktarov, who had won the UFC 6 tournament by defeating Tank Abbott in the finals. Unfortunately for UFC fans at that time, Shamrock versus Taktarov did not live up to its hype, as the two fighters battled to the thirty-three-minute time limit, and, since there still were no ringside judges, the fight was declared a draw. Shamrock's long draw with Royce Gracie and now this fight, which was equally long and very dull, garnered Shamrock a reputation for being a fighter who fought a slower-paced style, which resulted in long and boring fights. The fight with Taktarov certainly wouldn't be the last Ken Shamrock fight to fall into the "boring" category.

Shamrock fought again for UFC at UFC 8—the fourth straight UFC show he fought on—which took place on February 16, 1996, in San Juan, Puerto Rico. Shamrock headlined the show, successfully defending the Superfight title against Kimo Leopoldo in Kimo's first fight back in UFC since he'd rocked Royce Gracie's world in the first round of the UFC 3 tournament a couple of years earlier. Shamrock was able to submit Kimo with a kneebar at 4:24 of the fight.

Since UFC 6 and the first Ultimate Ultimate in December 1995, UFC buy-rates, although still quite high, had started to slip. The peak for UFC buyrates was a 1.05 for UFC 5 (headlined by Shamrock versus Royce Gracie), a 1.1 for UFC 6, and a 1.0 for the 1995 Ultimate Ultimate. UFC 7 had dropped down below the 1.0 mark with a 0.9 buyrate, and UFC 8 dropped even further down the ladder to a 0.7. The main reasons for this were that, when UFC first came out, it was unique because no one had ever seen something like this before, but after this many events it was no longer a unique concept. Royce Gracie had left the company without ever actually losing a match, which damaged the product, because many fans would forever see him as the top star who had never returned. Ken Shamrock's inability to defeat Royce at UFC 5 had cost the UFC dearly in retrospect, because had he been able to get the visual of his arm being raised at the end of that bout instead of going to the draw and getting the moral victory, then fans would've seen him as top dog in the promotion. But they didn't, and although Shamrock was still a mega-draw and a true headline fighter, Royce's leaving the company, combined with Shamrock's dull matches, for the most part damaged the UFC's box office.

And things were about to get a whole lot worse. Dan Severn had come back from his loss to Shamrock at UFC 6 to win the first Ultimate Ultimate tournament—considered up to that point in time the biggest tournament in MMA history—by defeating Paul Varelans, Tank Abbott, and Oleg Taktarov in one night. Severn looked great by winning the tournament, and although the general feeling about Severn was that he didn't have the charisma or superstar presence to be a headliner, SEG felt that they had no choice: with Severn's win of the Ultimate Ultimate, they'd have to give him a shot at the Superfight title still held by Ken Shamrock. Severn versus Shamrock II was then booked for UFC 9 at Cobo Hall in Detroit on May 17, 1996.

The fight was a disaster. SEG President Bob Meyrowitz had spent the day of the fight in court with UFC head referee John McCarthy and a team of lawyers because the district attorney of Michigan was trying to shut UFC 9 down. The event nearly didn't happen until the Michigan judge ruled that the show could indeed go on, as long as there were no headbutts and no closed-fist strikes to the head. According to this deal, SEG would fine a fighter fifty dollars for each infraction of these new rules specific to this event, but for most of the fights on the card, it's not like the fighters stopped using closed fists or anything.

Ken Shamrock had suffered a broken jaw in training, and had two bruised ribs and a dislocated knee going into the fight. The new rules for the event handed down by the Michigan courts had thrown Shamrock off, and in a scene reminiscent of when Shamrock didn't want to come out to fight Manabu Yamada in the King of Pancrase title tournament finals years earlier, it took a lot of convincing from Bob Shamrock, Bob Meyrowitz, and SEG official David Isaacs to get Shamrock to come out for the title fight against Severn.

He might as well have just stayed in the dressing room and let Severn go out there to fight an imaginary fighter, because the fight would go down as one of the worst, if not *the* worst, fight in MMA history. Both fighters spent the entire first fifteen minutes of the bout just dancing around each other; Shamrock stood in the middle of the octagon, and Severn circled him.

Neither fighter did anything. Severn's game plan was to go out there and do nothing and wait for Shamrock to react to him. Severn figured that Shamrock was a guy who preferred to react to the other fighter rather than making his own move first, so if he did nothing, neither would Shamrock, and the booing fans would get to Shamrock psychologically. It was an interesting game plan, but it made for a terribly boring fight. However, Severn was able to open a cut on Shamrock during the fight, and against the wishes of SEG, the judges ruled Severn the victor of the bout and the new UFC Superfight champion.

The fight was such a disaster for business that SEG never booked Severn again when he was champion until they put him against Mark Coleman in a fight Severn didn't have a chance of winning. Shamrock's image was greatly damaged with the fans: the biggest star of the promotion, he basically went out there and didn't fight. On top of all of that, even with all the hype for the main event, the show only drew a 0.65 rating, down from UFC 8, and UFC 10 saw an even larger drop-off in business, drawing just a 0.43 buyrate.

"[Severn and I] fought again, and he won a decision that was a terrible fight for both sides. It was a terrible fight," says Shamrock on his fight with Severn at UFC 9. "No one did anything. I had injuries that I was trying to get away from, and they set down the rules that there was no punching, but they allowed punching anyways, and they'd just fine you at a later date. I thought it was wrong. I went in to fight anyways because of the pressure I was under to take the fight, but I had a cracked rib and a lateral meniscus tear and a broken nose, and I had all these things that happened a few weeks before the event, but I went in there and fought anyways, even though they took away punches, and that was all I was able to do with the injuries that I had. And they said go ahead and punch anyways, and we'll fine you, and you can pay it whenever you want. And I said, 'No, this is the sanctioned rules set down by Detroit.' I didn't feel right about it. I went in there, and I fought Severn, and I didn't punch, and I lost the decision because I was fighting at half of what I should've been."

Realistically, as top fighters and stars, Shamrock and Severn were both toast. Severn would only fight twice more (the fight in which he lost the title to Coleman, and then years later, against Pedro Rizzo as a last-minute replacement for another fighter) for UFC, and Shamrock would only do one more fight for the company during this period of time.

Shamrock's return to the octagon, his final UFC fight for many years, was at the 1996 Ultimate Ultimate, where he took on Brian Johnston in the first round. The '96 Ultimate Ultimate was even more stacked with superstar fighters than the first version of the tournament a year earlier, and one of the big fights that people wanted to see on the card was Ken against Tank Abbott, as the two had been in a war of words throughout the year and people wanted to see their feud get settled. SEG booked Shamrock and Tank against different first-round opponents, the idea being that the two would meet in the second round.

However, that didn't happen. Tank defeated his first-round opponent, Cal Worsham, in 2:51. Shamrock was also able to get past Brian Johnston by submitting him with a choke in 5:48, but in the process Shamrock broke his hand and had to pull out of the tournament. There would be no Tank Abbott versus Ken Shamrock, as this was Shamrock's final UFC fight.

With the UFC's popularity winding down, the buyrates on pay-per-view not as successful as they had been a couple of years earlier, and political pressure setting in (pressure that would soon thereafter throw UFC off cable and realistically bury the promotion for a number of years), UFC didn't have the money to afford top superstar fighters like Ken Shamrock. Even though Shamrock had been damaged as a draw by the Severn fight at UFC 9, there were still many promoters, mostly in pro wrestling, interested in using him and willing to pay more for his services than UFC could offer.

"When I was [in UFC under SEG], I packed the houses and had the biggest pay-per-view rates, and I had one fight that was a letdown, and that was the Severn fight [at UFC 9]," says Shamrock on his initial run with UFC. "But the letdown I believe was that the office failed us, with the fact that when the rules were set down we were told that we could break them [at UFC 9], and I thought that was wrong. But other than that, I've always gone out and fought and did my best, and I've always been a fan favorite. The fans have always followed me, and it pays off if you see the way the fans follow me over the years."

Shamrock had been negotiating with New Japan Pro Wrestling at that time, but when a better offer came along from Vince McMahon's World Wrestling Federation, he ended up signing that contract instead, jumping ship to the WWF.

"We had been talking with New Japan, and they put me on a card, but we never had a deal then, and we never even said we were gonna do a deal, we just said it sounded good," says Shamrock. "I was negotiating at the time with WCW, WWF, and New Japan because UFC and [SEG President] Bob Meyrowitz, were having trouble, and they weren't able to pay me the money that was guaranteed to me. And I said I understand your problems, Bob Meyrowitz, and I wish I could help you out, but I have a family to support, and I need to find an area where I can make enough money to support my family. So we left on good terms, but at that time we were negotiating with three different companies, and WWF came up with the best offer, and that's where I went."

Shamrock debuted with the company in early 1997. He appeared before more than 18,000 fans at WrestleMania 13 on March 23, 1997, at the Horizon arena in Chicago, guest referee for one of the most legendary WWF matches of all time: Bret Hart versus Steve Austin. Many credit this match with offering one of the biggest boosts to Steve Austin's superstar status, and many feel this was the greatest match in WrestleMania history.

Shamrock had been brought into the WWF when Bret Hart, one of the most popular and most athletic wrestlers in the company at the time, convinced the WWF office that a good idea would be to build a feud between himself and Shamrock around the WWF World championship, because Shamrock's reputation as a real fighter would bring a feeling of legitimacy and respect to the title, and on top of that Hart enjoyed working a more "realistic" and mat-based style of pro wrestling. Hart wasn't the WWF champion at the time, but he was under the impression that he was going to get a lengthy run with the title and thought that Shamrock, with his submissions wrestling background, would be the perfect opponent to work a long feud around that style. Shamrock went to Calgary, Hart's hometown, to tune up his skills in pro wrestling, training under Hart and another Calgary-based pro wrestler named Leo Burke.

The proposed Hart-Shamrock feud never came to fruition, as Hart was ousted from the WWF in late '97 due to a political situation with Vince McMahon, and Shamrock spent most of his WWF run as a mid-level talent, albeit a mid-level talent during the biggest boom period of pro wrestling popularity in the history of the industry. A couple of the more notable pro wrestling matches of Shamrock's stay with WWF include the time Shamrock headlined a pay-per-view titled "D-Generation X" in December 1997 against then–WWF World champion Shawn Michaels, and a match with The Rock over the WWF Intercontinental title at WrestleMania 14 at the Fleet Center on March 29, 1998, during The Rock's meteoric rise in wrestling. Shamrock also held the Intercontinental title back when that title belt was considered the second most important in the promotion. UFC tried to negotiate to bring Shamrock back for one bout at their debut show in Japan to take on legendary Japanese pro wrestler Nobuhiko Takada in the main event of the show, but Takada wanted Shamrock to lose in a worked bout for him, and WWF wasn't going to allow Shamrock to do a worked loss in another promotion. Overall, Shamrock's run in WWF lasted close to thirty months.

"I think WWF did everything they promised me," says Shamrock on his WWF success. "They took care of me in there, and they pushed me. I went over a lot of people."

Shamrock had suffered a neck injury in late 1999, and had been on the WWF's disabled list for a while until PRIDE came along and offered him a deal to go back to the world of MMA and fight for them in Japan.

"I hurt my neck and was on the road quite a bit, and I was getting burnt out, and I wanted to step back and take a break, and when I got hurt I was out for a few months, and WWF let go of my contract," recalls Shamrock. "When they did, at that time I went ahead and made a deal with PRIDE."

Shamrock hadn't fought in MMA since his last UFC appearance in December 1996, and now, more than three years later, not only had MMA techniques advanced considerably, but Shamrock's body had also taken a lot of abuse from his years in WWF. Born to fight, Shamrock took PRIDE up on the offer, and signed the contract.

Shamrock made his return to the world of MMA on May 1, 2000, at the Tokyo Dome, for the PRIDE Grand Prix tournament finals. PRIDE, behind the box-office drawing power of native hero Kazushi Sakuraba, had become one of the biggest promotions in Japan and easily the biggest MMA-rules promotion in history, and had staged a two-night, sixteen-man tournament in 2000 featuring some of the biggest names and best fighters in the industry. Shamrock did not compete in the tournament, but instead fought pro wrestler-turned-mixed martial artist Alexander Otsuka in a special attraction match.

This show was the first PRIDE pay-per-view to air in North America, as it featured the two biggest drawing cards in U.S. MMA history: Ken Shamrock was back for his first fight in years, and Royce Gracie took on Kazushi Sakuraba in what was only his second fight in 2000 (Gracie's first fight had been against Nobuhiko Takada in the first round of the Grand Prix tournament earlier in the year). It was the most important show in company history until then, a distinction it may still hold to this day.

Otsuka was generally considered a poor fighter but a tough guy, one who worked very hard to entertain the fans, his gimmick being that he would use pro wrestling moves in MMA fights. This, of course, never really worked out for him, but it was entertaining nonetheless. He was the perfect opponent for Shamrock's return as, due to Shamrock's age, accumulated injuries, and the overall advancement of techniques in MMA, it was questionable whether Shamrock could continue to fight top talent. Fighting Otsuka first would most likely give Shamrock a fairly easy and exciting victory.

Shamrock was able to knock Otsuka out in the match in impressive fashion, and his return to MMA and his PRIDE debut were both considered successful.

Shamrock's next fight in PRIDE took place on August 27, 2000, on PRIDE 10, where he faced another Japanese pro wrestler-turned-mixed martial artist in Kazuyuki Fujita. Unlike Otsuka, though, Fujita was a fighter considered to have some skill, especially in wrestling, and had a reputation for being able to take a hard blow to the head, so it was unlikely that Shamrock, never known for his standup skills, would be able to knock Fujita out like he had Otsuka.

Although Shamrock was able to dominate Fujita during the early part of the fight, Shamrock had a disappointing outing and started to gas out a few minutes into the bout. When Fujita managed to bull Shamrock into the corner, he signaled that he wanted to stop the fight. Shamrock clearly wasn't conditioned for the bout, and, as MMA history has shown happens to fighters who don't condition properly, a major upset occurred, and Fujita walked away the winner.

Shamrock's next MMA fight didn't happen for another year. He would do one of the only traditional-style pro wrestling matches in Japan of his career on New Year's Eve 2000 when he teamed with Don Frye to wrestle Nobuhiko Takada and Keiji Mutoh. Some of Shamrock's other notable high-profile traditional-style pro wrestling matches in Japan were against Vader at an FMW show, and against Takashi Iizuka at a New Japan show at the Tokyo Dome in May of 2003.

Shamrock was booked for the third fight of his PRIDE career at the March 25, 2001, show against highly skilled striker Igor Vovchanchyn. Just prior to the bout, however, Shamrock managed to aggravate an old neck injury, so fellow Lion's Den member Tra Telligman took his place. With his boxing skills, Telligman was able to upset Vovchanchyn to win the decision. It was also rumored that Shamrock would fight Mark Coleman during this period of time, but that fight never ended up happening either.

Shamrock's neck injury ended up keeping him out of MMA competition for a number of months. He made his return on August 10, 2001, on MegaFight, a show that he promoted himself at the Tropicana Casino in Atlantic City. There he quickly submitted journeyman fighter Sam Adkins at 1:26 of the first round in the card's main event with a Kimura.

On February 24, 2002, at PRIDE 19, the grudge match between Shamrock and Frye finally took place. Their feud had now been simmering for a couple of years. This was the final fight booked on Shamrock's three-fight contract with PRIDE, for a rumored $350,000 per fight, and he needed the big win over Frye to get a renewal. There was a lot of money at stake in this bout.

The fight would live up to its hype, for the most part, as both fighters went out to the ring and waged war on one another until Frye pulled out a split-decision victory—although the fight was realistically too close to call. The fight was hell on both fighters, as Frye destroyed his knees and ankles during the bout. Shamrock's contract with PRIDE wasn't renewed, and because Frye had pulled off the judges' decision, he continued to fight in major matches for PRIDE.

"The Don Frye fight in Japan was huge, it was big, and it even got recognized here in the United States," says Shamrock. "I fought the best I could, and I thought I did more damage to him than he did to me."

The show was also a success business-wise in the United States, where PRIDE pay-per-views weren't very popular, since most of the fighters on the shows weren't well known to the American casual audience, and the audience wasn't aware that many fighters that they did know (Shamrock being an example) were even in the promotion. PRIDE 19, though, behind the Frye versus Shamrock hype, ended up doing significantly better on U.S. pay-per-view than any PRIDE show had done in the past.

This pay-per-view success foreshadowed events to come, as upon exiting PRIDE, Shamrock had entered into negotiations with both UFC and WWE (formerly WWF). Although he hovered around the age of forty by this point in his career, Shamrock did not want to leave the world of competition and go back to pro wrestling full time, and WWE wasn't interested in him unless he was exclusive to their promotion. In 2002, Shamrock signed a contract to return to the promotion that made him famous in the U.S.: the UFC.

Shamrock's first fight back in UFC was the now-legendary fight against Tito Ortiz on November 22, 2002, at the MGM Grand Casino in Las Vegas. Ken's dislike for Tito was no secret within MMA circles. The two had had a confrontation on March 5, 1999, at UFC 19 after Ortiz defeated Shamrock protégé Guy Mezger, whom Shamrock had cornered for the bout. Ortiz put on a T-shirt that read, "Gay Mezger Is My Bitch," and got into a verbal confrontation with Shamrock until referee John McCarthy pulled Tito away. Ortiz had made it clear that he did not like and had no respect for the Lion's Den fighters, having also defeated Jerry Bohlander in an earlier fight.

Shamrock's return to the UFC was a very big deal, and it brought back many of the mid-'90s fans who had tuned out when he and other "name" fighters had left the promotion (which was largely because of the cable ban on MMA shows established in early 1997). The cable ban had since been lifted, and the UFC had been sold to the Fertitta brothers in January 2001. Under the ownership of the Fertittas, Shamrock versus Ortiz at UFC 40 would draw the most buys on pay-per-view at roughly 150,000. Although it was short of the record pay-per-view buyrates set for the promotion in the 1990s, it was way beyond anything that the promotion had ever done under the ownership of the Fertittas. The show also set the record for paid attendance and gate for the UFC: 13,055 fans paid for a gate in excess of $1.5 million.

"I think people can feel my charisma and the realness of my anger and the realness of when I get in a fight," says Shamrock about why he's been such a box-office drawing card in MMA. "When I step in the ring, people like to watch me fight because I don't hold back. I go in there and I cut loose and I fight, and my fights are exciting, and I'm not afraid to fight, and I'm not afraid to speak my mind when it comes to interviews, and when someone pisses me off I don't have a problem getting in their face. But I don't make stuff up. It's not made up, it's real."

Tito and Ken had appeared on Fox SportsNet's *Best Damn Sports Show, Period* to hype up the fight. The fight itself, beyond the story line grudge between Tito and Ken, wasn't anything special: Ortiz dominated Shamrock until Shamrock gave up after the third round due to the degree of punishment he was taking in the bout. But the hype and story line behind the fight made it more exciting than anything else could have; what makes a great match both in terms of quality and in terms of selling pay-per-views and tickets are unique personalities in an important matchup. Ken Shamrock and Tito Ortiz are two of the most unique personalities in MMA, and the combination of the hype for the fight, their real-life grudge, and the fact that the UFC Light-Heavyweight title was also on the line made for an important bout, and a successful show.

"I brought the UFC from doing 40,000 buys to 150,000 buys," Shamrock comments on the subject of his return to UFC in the Tito Ortiz fight. "I made a huge impact coming back, and a lot of it had to do with taking fights that mean something. Tito Ortiz, I hated him. Don Frye, he opened his mouth and said some things, but we're good now, and we're friends now. But prior to that we had some problems. But I'm able to take these things and really bring them out and create some heat and some anger because I have to be angry when I fight. That's just the way I fight. And by doing that the fans get into it more. I don't do it to set it up or create it, it's just me. It's what I do.

I think I made a huge impact, and even though I didn't win the fights [with Frye in PRIDE and Tito in UFC], they were huge fights. I did everything I could to win them, but under the circumstances and under the position that I was in I wasn't able to do the things I needed to. But I was able to make the fight good."

Although Shamrock and Ortiz disliked each other, it was clearly a passing-of-the-torch deal: a legend from yesteryear came back and was defeated by the modern champion.

"Well, you know everyone has excuses, and I do not have one. I got beat, bottom line," Shamrock concedes.

Shamrock had moved down to the Light-Heavyweight division to take the fight, and moved back up to Heavyweight afterward. He was booked against undercard fighter Ian Freeman at UFC 43 on June 2003 in a heavyweight matchup, but Ken injured his ACL in training and had to pull out of the match and take a few months off.

"You know you have to be 100 percent to step into the ring anymore, there is just no question. You have to be 100 percent going in," says Shamrock. "Obviously there are little things you have to overcome in training, and things of that nature. You can't go in there being limited on your abilities; otherwise you are not going to come out on top."

Now that he's past the age of forty, the end of Shamrock's career may or may not be far off. "When do you tell a guy he has to retire? Each guy is different," says Shamrock. "What if I'm out there beating guys when I'm forty-five years old, do I retire because I'm forty-five, or do I retire because I'm done? I think you have to take a look at each individual, and [they must] have willpower and train hard and keep training hard and keep competing at a high level and still be able to compete at a high level, and when they get into the ring and fight top fighters and not embarrass themselves, and I think as long as they are able to do that . . . age is just a number. I think it depends on a person's will and a person's ability, and if they are able to go in there and fight top guys and do well then there's no reason that they should retire if they are hungry."

In November 2003, at UFC's tenth anniversary show, Shamrock was honored as one of two charter members of the UFC Hall of Fame (the other being Royce Gracie).

But just because he was in the UFC's Hall of Fame doesn't mean he was done competing. Shamrock would make his return to the octagon in June 2004 in a rematch against Kimo Leopoldo, although UFC had originally wanted to book Shamrock against Tank Abbott in a payoff to the war of words that had occurred between the two during the past decade, but Tank set his price too high for that one match.

It was a good fight for Shamrock, because he was heavily favored to defeat Kimo. And he did just that, knocking Kimo out with one knee.

What happens to the pro wrestling and mixed martial arts legend after this point in his MMA career is uncertain, but he will always remain an icon in both the UFC and mixed martial arts as a whole.

Royce Gracie

There is an athlete at the pinnacle of every sport, an athlete whose name has become synonymous with the sport he plays due to all that he has accomplished. These athletes often end up becoming larger than the sport itself. In baseball there is Babe Ruth. In hockey there is Wayne Gretzky. In basketball there is Michael Jordan. And, for the UFC, there is Royce Gracie.

No one in mixed martial arts has had more influence over the modern world of the sport than Royce Gracie. He was at the forefront of the development of an exciting, new sport. He completely changed the entire world's perspective on what works and what doesn't in a reality fighting situation. He was the initial icon of the UFC, and the biggest box-office draw the promotion had for its early events. Ten years after his debut in UFC, he still is recognized worldwide as a high-caliber athlete in the sport.

Royce was born on December 12, 1966, in Rio de Janeiro, Brazil. He was the sixth son of Helio Gracie, who was possibly the most influential member of the most legendary fighting family in martial arts history, the Gracies. Helio is one of the greatest figures in martial arts history, having founded one of the most vital martial arts on the planet early last century, Gracie Jiu Jitsu, after his older brother Carlos trained him in the Japanese art of jujutsu.

Jujutsu (different from jiu jitsu) was actually a name that encompassed hundreds of different styles of martial arts in Japan, where the arts were passed down from generation to generation over the course of many centuries. One expert in Japan may have just taught standing and striking and referred to it as jujutsu, whereas another may have taught only grappling and called it the same thing, so there were many variants of the art.

Mitsuyo Maeda, a jujutsu expert, also learned Kodokan Judo from that sport's founder, Jigoro Kano, in the early 1900s, when judo was just in development. Maeda traveled around Japan and later throughout Europe, fighting in exhibition martial arts and working pro wrestling matches. He actually may have picked up some knowledge of catch-as-catch-can wrestling (wrestling with striking and submissions) throughout his travels, in addition to what he learned in Japan.

Maeda eventually wound up in Brazil, where he befriended an influential foreign services officer named Gastao Gracie, who was of Brazilian and Scottish descent. Gracie helped to secure a consulate post for Maeda, and Maeda assisted in bringing Japanese settlers to Brazil. In exchange for Gracie's help, Maeda offered to teach Gracie's eldest son, Carlos, the art of jujutsu.

Carlos, in turn, taught all of his younger siblings. All of them, that is, except Helio, who was not taught the art directly because, still young, he was always very sick and frail, and the family thought that the art might not mix well with his weakened state.

Well, they were wrong. Carlos opened up a dojo in Rio de Janeiro and began to teach students, and Helio watched and learned from the sidelines. According to the myth, one of Carlos's students showed up to the school for a lesson one day, but Carlos wasn't around, so Helio, who was there, offered to start the class until Carlos got there. Carlos didn't show up until the class was over, and found that the student was more impressed with Helio and wanted to train under him from then on. It was at that point that Helio edited through what Maeda had taught Carlos, keeping what worked and throwing out what didn't, ultimately creating the art of Gracie Jiu Jitsu as it is known today.

Helio went on to compete in many jiu jitsu and vale tudo (Brazilian term for mixed martial arts) bouts during his career, and became a tabloid celebrity in Brazil. He also taught his many sons the art. When Helio's oldest son, Rorion, grew up, he decided to travel to the United States to help spread his father's art. Rorion found living in the U.S. hard at first, as he was basically homeless in California when he first arrived. Eventually, he began to train students out of his garage.

In 1989, *Playboy* magazine ran an article, entitled "Bad," on Rorion Gracie. The article caught the eye of an advertising executive, Art Davie, who lived in Los Angeles at the time. A boxing fan, Davie had established himself as a successful ad man and entrepreneur. He ended up visiting Rorion's new school, and they became friends. Davie helped Rorion promote a series of videotapes called *Gracies in Action*, which featured fights involving various Gracie family members. The tapes sold very well, and the reaction in the martial arts community was enthusiastic, so Davie came up with a concept for a promotion based on this style of fighting, and on the concept of taking martial artists from many popular styles (i.e., karate, judo, tae kwon do, etc.) and putting them all into a one-night tournament to see which fighter and which style would come out on top. This idea eventually evolved into the Ultimate Fighting Championship.

The UFC found a pay-per-view backer in Bob Meyrowitz's Semaphore Entertainment Group (SEG, which would later become the principal owner of the company), and the format for the first UFC event was established. It would be an eight-man, one-night tournament, with as few rules as possible, and a grand prize of $50,000 would go to the winner.

Originally, Rickson Gracie, then known as the best fighter in the Gracie family, was picked by the Gracies to represent both their family and the sport, but family politics got in the way. Rickson had been teaching students on the side, and Rorion didn't approve, so the family decided that Royce would represent them in the inaugural UFC event.

Royce had grown up in Brazil, but he moved to California to live with Rorion in 1984, at age seventeen. Born into a fighting family, he had been training in Gracie Jiu Jitsu his entire life, and although he was young, just over six feet tall, and weighed only 180 pounds at the time of the first UFC tournament, his family had the utmost confidence that he would succeed.

Royce started competing in Brazilian Jiu Jitsu tournaments at eight years of age, and received his blue belt in jiu jitsu at sixteen. Two years later, he received his black belt in the Gracies' trademark martial art. When he first moved to California to live with Rorion, he began to train people in Rorion's garage, sometimes up to ten hours a day. This lasted until they opened a school in Torrance, California, a short while before the first UFC event.

Royce spent his days building up to the first UFC event on November 12, 1993, in a rigid training program designed to get him into top physical shape for the night of action. Since Rorion Gracie had invested in the UFC, he had a degree of control over the placement of the fighters and over who was matched up against whom. Royce was put up against professional boxer Art Jimmerson, as Rorion obviously figured that he could prove the dominance of Gracie Jiu Jitsu over the mainstream sport of boxing early in the night.

Jimmerson was ranked in the top ten for the WBC Cruiserweight title in the late 1980s after winning *Ring Magazine*'s Fight of the Year award for his knockout win against Lenny LaPaglia at Madison Square Garden in 1988. Jimmerson, who knew the score when it comes to grappling versus boxing (as most boxers do), was not easily convinced to come fight in the UFC, and ended up being paid $20,000—the highest guarantee of the night—just to enter the tournament.

In the third fight of the night, in front of 2,800 surprised fans at McNichols Arena in Denver, Royce made very quick work of Jimmerson. Jimmerson came out wearing a boxing glove on one hand (which looked ridiculous), and he clearly wanted no part of the no-holds-barred action—he submitted immediately as Royce took him down to the canvas of the octagon and delivered one headbutt.

This win advanced Royce into the tournament's semifinals, where he came up against one of his biggest career rivals and one of the biggest names in MMA history: Ken Shamrock.

Shamrock had three fights' worth of experience under his belt for Pancrase in Japan, and had fought in Pancrase just four days before the first UFC event. When Shamrock arrived in Colorado with his hulking bodybuilder's frame, submission fighting skill, and experience in Pancrase, many of the martial arts experts on hand for the event figured he was the surefire winner of the eight-man tournament.

On one side of the octagon was Shamrock's chiseled figure, and on the other side stood the puny Royce Gracie, preparing to battle.

During the fight, when Shamrock went for an ankle lock, Gracie wasted no time in getting in position for a rear naked choke. Shamrock tapped out. The referee didn't see it at first, but after some prodding from Royce, Shamrock acknowledged to the ref that he had given in, and the bout was over.

"He never understood how a little guy like me could beat him," commented Royce on Shamrock's reaction to the fight in UFC's *Ultimate Royce Gracie* video. David had defeated Goliath.

"You've got this Adonis god–looking guy walking in to destroy this skinny little guy from Brazil," says mixed martial arts promoter and former UFC broadcaster Jeff Osborne, "and the little guy beat him. There's nothing like a good movie where the little guy beats the big guy. And that's what he did."

Royce was the victor of this fight, but it wasn't the last time Royce and Shamrock would come face to face in the octagon. It also wasn't the last fight of the night, since Royce had now advanced to the finals of the tournament, to take on Dutch savate expert Gerard Gordeau.

Gordeau was a roughneck kickboxer from Holland, a country known for producing tons of top-tier kickboxing talent. He had defeated sumo Teila Tuli and another kickboxer, Kevin Rosier, to make it to the tournament finals. The finals didn't last long, as Royce quickly took Gordeau down and the Dutchman rolled onto his stomach, leaving himself wide open for the rear naked choke, which Gracie applied to win the fight and the tournament.

In one night, Royce had not only put the UFC on the map as a popular pay-per-view promotion, he had not only become the first true superstar of a new fighting sport, he had not only popularized the gi and grappling and made jiu jitsu a household term, but he had also revolutionized what people imagined would work in a reality fighting situation. Royce had proven that a good grappler would defeat a good boxer or kickboxer nearly every time, because once the grappler took the striker to the mat, there was nothing more a striker could do but lose.

"It will open everybody's eyes, especially the weaker guys, that you don't have to be a monster to be the champ," Royce commented on the *Ultimate Royce* video after winning that first UFC tournament. "You don't have to be the biggest guy or the one who hits the hardest. And you don't have to get hurt in a fight."

"At the start, nobody outside of Brazil or a Gracie studio thought he would win," said longtime UFC referee John McCarthy on the *Ultimate Royce* video. "Martial arts as we know it today has changed because of Royce and what he first did ten years ago."

The initial UFC event was successful enough that they decided to return to the idea and run UFC 2 again in Denver, but this time at the smaller Mammoth Gardens because political opposition (to the perceived violence of UFC) kept them from running it in a larger arena. The UFC tournament format was increased from an eight-man tournament to a sixteen-man tournament, meaning that the eventual tournament winner would have to fight four times in one night to earn the winner's purse.

The majority of the first-round fights took place before the pay-per-view started to broadcast, although Royce's first-round fight with Minoki Ichihara did air on the pay-per-view. Royce was able to submit the karate master in just over five minutes—again proving the dominance of grappling against standup fighting, and positioning himself to move on to the second round. That first fight would turn out to have been Royce's longest of the night.

In the second round, Royce came up against an opponent he was very familiar with, Jason DeLucia. DeLucia was a journeyman martial arts expert who had fought Royce in a dojo challenge match that had been taped and marketed on one of the *Gracies in Action* videotapes. In that fight, DeLucia had thought he would have been able to defeat Gracie with his knowledge of the traditional striking-based martial arts, but Royce had easily taken him down and tapped him out. DeLucia wanted to fight Royce in the first UFC, but since all of the slots were full, he'd had to wait until this event. At UFC 2, DeLucia would get another crack at Royce.

Yet again proving the dominance of jiu jitsu over traditional and standup martial arts, Royce was able to armbar and submit DeLucia just over a minute into the fight, after DeLucia broke his fibula delivering a kick to Royce's shin.

This win sent Royce to the semifinals of that night's tournament, where Royce took on another jiu jitsu expert for the first time in his UFC career: Remco Pardoel, who had won jiu jitsu championships in four different countries. Not only was Pardoel a jiu jitsu expert, but he also had a weight advantage of over 100 pounds on Royce, so logic suggests that Pardoel would easily beat Royce at his own game.

Instead, in another incidence of David defeating Goliath, Royce took Pardoel down, and found that Pardoel was less versed in groundfighting than he was, and proceeded to choke him out in less than ninety seconds.

In this fight, Gracie had proven that not only could he defeat standup fighters and traditional martial artists with his Gracie Jiu Jitsu background, but that even other martial artists from a different field of grappling couldn't compete with Gracie and his family's martial art at this point in time. The win over Pardoel also proved that Royce's success was not just because of the fight technique he employed, but also due to his burning desire to win, even against another bigger and skilled grappler.

This again launched Royce into the UFC tournament finals, pitting him against kickboxer and general bad boy Patrick Smith.

Gracie again proved the dominance of groundfighting in this early UFC event, as the fight was done in just over a minute. Gracie managed to take Smith down and get into full mount, and Smith, feeling that there wasn't anything else to do, tapped out.

"Over here [Smith] is telling me, 'Good job baby, good job baby,'" Royce recalls in the *Ultimate Royce* video. "I knee him, as soon as I do that, he was like 'That was good baby, keep going baby.' He was coaching. I was like 'What is wrong with this guy? He's coaching me through the fight against him.'"

By defeating four other fighters in one night to win the second UFC tournament and the $60,000 grand prize, Royce Gracie proved to the world yet again that Gracie Jiu Jitsu—and groundfighting in general—reigned supreme. Royce was able to defeat these four other men so quickly that the total amount of time he spent fighting over the course of the four bouts that night was just under nine minutes.

UFC 3 was a very interesting event; it was the first time that Royce showed any weakness in the octagon. The show, which cut its tournament format down from sixteen men back to eight men, had been built around the hype of Royce Gracie and Ken Shamrock possibly meeting in the finals. Shamrock had not fought in UFC since losing to Royce at the first UFC event nearly a year earlier, but he had continued to fight in the Pancrase organization in Japan, and wanted another run at the small Brazilian man who had made him tap their first time out.

Buyrates continued to climb for the UFC events. The first show drew roughly 80,000 buys, and UFC 3, based around the hype of a possible Shamrock-Royce rematch in the tournament finals, nearly doubled that total.

Fate had different plans for this night, though. In the first round of the tournament, Royce came up against a mysterious Hawaiian fighter named Kimo, who rocked Royce's world by giving him the most competitive match of his career up to that point in time. Kimo was quite the sight, walking to the ring carrying a cross on his back à la Jesus Christ, with the word "Jesus" tattooed across his stomach—and that was only one of many tattoos on the very muscular frame of the Hawaiian bad man. Royce had his work cut out for him that night.

With a tremendous strength advantage over the smaller Royce, Kimo was able to outpower him in one of the most exciting fights from the early period of UFC history. They battled around the ring, Kimo using his raw, unskilled strength, and Royce using the finesse and the ultra-skill of Gracie Jiu Jitsu in an attempt to keep Kimo at bay, and further to try to defeat him.

At one point in the four-minute fight, Kimo nearly sank in a choke on Royce, but his lack of skill prevented that from happening, and Royce was able to armbar and submit Kimo. It was an exhausting fight for both men.

"I won that fight with pure technique after the first two minutes," Royce continues. "After the first two minutes, the strength, endurance, was all gone."

Gracie's second-round opponent was to be Harold Howard, but the fight never happened, since Royce's corner threw in the towel after Royce came to the octagon, but before the fight got started. The fight against Kimo had exhausted Royce, and he'd hit the wall. There was no way that he could continue to fight in the physical state he was in.

This was a huge disappointment for the fans, since it was the first UFC tournament that Royce did not win—he didn't even compete in the finals. Even more disappointed, however, was Ken Shamrock, who had returned to the UFC for one reason: to get a rematch with Royce Gracie. And that was the fight that fans wanted to see. But after he defeated Christophe Leninger and Felix Lee Mitchell in the first two rounds of the tournament, Shamrock pulled out of the finals, claiming an ankle injury. But the biggest reason he didn't go out there for the finals was that the man on the opposite side of the octagon wouldn't be Royce Gracie, so Shamrock couldn't exact his revenge.

Shamrock would not be back to compete at UFC 4, since he continued to fight for Pancrase, but Royce would fight in his fourth straight tournament, taking on middle-aged former kung fu movie star Ron Van Clief in the first round. Gracie was able to take down and submit Van Clief in less than five minutes, and he advanced to the tournament's semifinals. There he defeated Keith Hackney (who went into the fight with an injured ankle) via armbar to make it to his third tournament finals in four UFC appearances.

His opponent for the finals wasn't just any average fighter, but former amateur wrestler Dan Severn, who had been one of the top collegiate-level amateur wrestlers in the early 1980s. This was his debut in the UFC, and in the best display of pure wrestling ability seen up to that point in the promotion's history, he suplexed Anthony Macias around the ring like a rag doll in his first-round fight—a clip that UFC keeps in their highlight reels to this day. Severn went into the finals with a well over seventy-pound weight advantage on Royce.

The fight with Severn was the longest of Royce's career up to that point, as they battled for over fifteen minutes before Royce was able to sink in a choke and get Severn to tap out.

This would prove to be Royce's last tournament in the UFC, as it was now time for Royce's rematch with Ken Shamrock. They were booked to fight at UFC 5. Instead of pitting Shamrock and Gracie in opposite brackets in the UFC 5 tournament, the UFC matchmakers decided that the best way to give the fans what they wanted was to pit Royce against Shamrock in a one-night "Superfight." The two would meet in the main event of UFC 5 for the newly created Superfight title (which would later become the Heavyweight title).

Ever since Royce's first encounter with Shamrock at the debut UFC event, fans had anxiously awaited another fight between the two. Behind Royce, buyrates for the UFC pay-per-views continued to soar to the level of major boxing and pro wrestling events, and people had taken notice of this new fighting promotion. UFC 5, built around Royce versus Shamrock II, would do approximately 260,000 buys on pay-per-view and a 1.05 buyrate, the highest in UFC history up to that point. To this day, it remains as one of the two most-watched UFC events of all time. The next event, UFC 6 with Ken Shamrock's first fight against Dan Severn, slightly surpassed the 260,000 mark with a 1.1 buyrate, just 0.05 higher than the buyrate for UFC 5.

Everyone wanted to see Gracie-Shamrock II. "Royce made you want to watch UFC," says Jeff Osborne. "You either tuned in to see Royce get his ass kicked or you tuned in to see him come out on top." But nobody wanted to see the fight that ended up taking place. Ken Shamrock had developed a reputation for being a guy who would sooner respond to techniques rather than initiate his own. When facing an opponent with a similar game plan, this approach can lead to a long and boring fight. Realistically, Royce Gracie was also a somewhat dull fighter, since practitioners of Brazilian Jiu Jitsu sometimes take a (long) while to defeat their opponents, but Royce had been successful as an exciting fighter because groundfighting was a new concept at the time, and he had been able to quickly submit his prior opponents.

Royce and Shamrock battled to a very unsatisfying thirty-six-minute draw. Most of the fight was spent on the ground, with Shamrock in Royce's guard, and both fighters were very inactive. "Suddenly a big guy like that was playing such a defensive game," said Royce in UFC's *Ultimate Royce* video about Shamrock's strategy for that fight. "Hey, if you gave me a forty-pound advantage, I'd tie one hand behind my back to fight him."

The live crowd, of course, booed the fight.

At one point in the bout, Shamrock was able to nail Gracie in the face with a punch that bloodied the Brazilian, and at other moments, he was active in offense in Gracie's guard.

Back then, UFC did not have ringside judges, so any fight that went to a time limit was declared a draw. Fans hated it, but that was the final verdict on Royce-Shamrock II. A draw is about the most anticlimactic ending possible for a major fight. The majority of MMA experts concede, however, that had there been ringside judges for the fight, then Shamrock would have won a clear-cut unanimous decision. Instead, Shamrock had to settle for the moral victory against Royce.

Royce felt differently about the outcome of the fight: "It was a draw. To me, personally, on the fight, it was a draw."

Royce would not take the opportunity to prove himself in the octagon again, though, since his rematch with Shamrock proved to be his final fight in UFC. Royce's older brother, Rorion, sold his shares in the UFC, not liking the frequent rule changes that the promotion started to invoke for their fights. Rorion had originally owned part of a limited liability company called War of the Worlds with Art Davie, and WOW had co-owned UFC with SEG. After UFC 5, SEG would become the sole owner of UFC until the company was completely sold to Zuffa, LLC, in January 2001.

Rorion had used Royce to prove the quality of his family's jiu jitsu to the world, and Royce had done just that in amazing fashion by winning three one-night tournaments. The Gracies felt that there was nothing else for him to accomplish that he hadn't already done, so logic said that it was time for Rorion to move on. Royce went with him, feeling that the numerous rule changes that were slowly being implemented in the UFC would change the promotion forever, and that all these new rules altered the fights so they weren't "realistic" enough. He didn't want to be a part of it. "[The fighters are] not fighting against each other. They're fighting against the clock," Royce commented in the *Martial Arts Gazette*. "[The fighters] don't come in to fight anymore; they come in for the draw. A lot of the fighters are playing for the draw. They're fighting for the judges. I'm sorry, I can't fight like that."

Royce, the biggest early star of the UFC, was the man who had made the promotion what it was, and his feud with Ken Shamrock remains arguably the most popular feud in UFC history, even ten years after their final confrontation. With Royce gone, and with Ken Shamrock as the main headliner against other opponents, UFC buyrates began to slip. UFC even tried to coax Royce into coming back by offering big money and rewards, but he wasn't interested in making another return to the promotion during that time.

Rorion Gracie had signed a two-year, no-compete clause after selling his shares in UFC to their pay-per-view company, SEG. Royce would also disappear from the mixed martial arts scene for a number of years, opting to compete in Brazilian Jiu Jitsu tournaments and teaching seminars and training programs in his chosen martial art.

Inside the world of martial arts, everyone agrees that Royce was the most influential martial artist of this generation. But Royce's success does prompt the question, would Royce's older brother Rickson, who was considered the superior fighter in the Gracie family when the UFC first started, have been able to accomplish what Royce did in the UFC? And if so, does this mean that, if Royce was so easily replaceable by another family member, it was the fighting style—not the fighter—that deserves credit for these accomplishments?

"I feel Rickson Gracie would have done as well, if not better, than Royce, because it is [or was] widely acknowledged within the Gracie family that Rickson is the best fighter in the family," says journalist and broadcaster Stephen Quadros. "Royce even stated in an interview that Rickson was 'ten times better' than him."

Quadros best sums up the topic by saying, "I don't think Royce's impact on MMA was lessened by the fact that he might have been replaceable by another family member. If anything, I feel it bolsters Royce's standing, because Rickson is perceived as superior to Royce. Because of that perception, Royce's achievements give me the impression that he rose to a new level, previously only thought attainable by Rickson. I feel it was his time to shine, and the fact remains that it was him, Royce, who fought in four UFC tournaments and dominated to win three of them."

Royce didn't compete in any other mixed martial arts events for a long while after he left UFC. His fame from fighting in UFC led to a lucrative business: Royce held martial arts seminars all across the globe and opened up a network of jiu jitsu schools throughout the United States and beyond.

Royce also continued to compete in Brazilian Jiu Jitsu during his time off. Jiu jitsu competitions are vastly different from mixed martial arts, as they are grappling-only, and if an athlete does well in jiu jitsu, it doesn't guarantee that he'll also do well in mixed martial arts (and vice versa). Jiu jitsu is just one martial art, whereas MMA is a kaleidoscope of them.

On December 17, 1998, Royce suffered his first loss in jiu jitsu. He was choked out at an event in Brazil by Wallid Ismael, a jiu jitsu master who has never done well in MMA. The loss sent shock waves through the martial arts world because of Royce's fame from the UFC, where no one had ever seen him lose.

Early in the fight, Royce made several poor defensive moves when Ismael was on the attack. About five minutes into the bout, Wallid was able to take Royce's back and lock in a choke. Royce briefly tried to get out of the hold, but he lost consciousness, and thereby lost the fight.

Although Royce never tapped to the choke, he wasn't broken up by the loss. "I congratulate Wallid on his victory. I will continue to train hard, and I look forward to fighting again soon," said Royce in a post-fight interview quoted in a Gracie Academy press release. Considering that the match was held under jiu jitsu rules and was not an MMA bout, and since only the most hardcore fans of martial arts would even know about it, the loss did little to damage Royce's unbeatable reputation in mixed martial arts.

By the time the year 2000 rolled around, it had been nearly five years since Royce's fight against Ken Shamrock at UFC 5—his final fight in either UFC or MMA. But that was about to change. In Japan, PRIDE had become a popular MMA promotion by catering to the country's large pro wrestling audience. UFC had fallen on hard times due to political pressure and had been forced off of cable. This meant that they weren't generating enough revenue to pay their "big name" fighters. So PRIDE picked up the slack by signing the biggest-name UFC fighters to fight in their organization.

PRIDE had decided to hold their first Grand Prix tournament in 2000. This promised to be the biggest tournament in mixed martial arts history to date, and they planned to sign up as many of the sport's big names as possible for the two-night, sixteen-man extravaganza. Royce would be among these sixteen fighters.

Many wondered whether Royce would be able to accomplish what he had done years ago in UFC in this new tournament. Mixed martial arts naturally evolves at a very fast rate, and even a fighter considered the best just a couple of years ago wouldn't necessarily do as well today, because the skill level of the fighters is constantly improving. Royce hadn't fought in nearly five years, and the sport had evolved so much in his time away that it was no longer the same thing that he had excelled at just a few years earlier in UFC.

"When I started, it was about proving which style was the best," Royce comments in the *Ultimate Royce* video regarding the evolution of mixed martial arts. "Today, it is about the fighter."

The tournament was split over two nights, with the first night featuring the opening round and the second night, months later, featuring the rest of the tournament. Royce's opponent for the first night of the tournament was Japanese pro wrestling legend Nobuhiko Takada. Takada was a natural opponent for Royce, because the concept of a Japanese fighter against a Gracie family member had become a major box-office draw in Japan. Takada had become a legendary hero in Japan as a pro wrestler in the early '90s, and had crossed over into MMA to fight Rickson Gracie at the very first PRIDE event in 1997.

Luckily for Royce, Takada was a terrible fighter and was only in PRIDE because, as a legendary pro wrestler, he had tremendous box-office drawing power. Takada is now retired from mixed martial arts competition, but nonetheless to this day he has never won what industry insiders consider to be a legitimate fight. The three wins on his record (against Kyle Sturgeon, pro wrestler Alexander Otsuka, and Mark Coleman) are all understood to be worked fights intended to put Takada over to the Japanese audience who, unaware that these wins were worked, would still have faith in their native hero.

On January 30, 2000, Royce made his return to the realm of mixed martial arts by defeating Takada via unanimous decision (as expected) in the final fight of the first night of the PRIDE Grand Prix in front of 48,316 people at the Tokyo Dome. The fight was actually long and dull, with Takada lying on top of Gracie, doing absolutely nothing, while Royce held him in the guard to eventually win the decision. Royce would now move on to the second round of the tournament, which was to be held on May 1, 2000.

Royce's opponent for the second round of the Grand Prix would be Japanese sensation Kazushi Sakuraba, who had defeated Guy Mezger in the first round of the tournament. Considered by many to be the most skilled Japanese fighter ever in MMA, and at that time one of the best pound-for-pound fighters in the sport, Sakuraba was Takada's protégé. He had come into PRIDE as a pro wrestler and made his name in the world of MMA by dominating Royce's younger brother Royler at PRIDE 8 in November 1999, in what was a landmark fight because no Gracie family member had ever lost under MMA rules up to that point. That fight is considered to be the one that put PRIDE on the map as a major promotion in Japan. Sakuraba's feud with the Gracie family became legendary in Japan, earning him the nickname of "The Gracie Hunter." Royce Gracie versus Kazushi Sakuraba was a natural matchup.

The Tokyo Dome was packed again for the second night of the tournament in May, with 38,000 people showing up to see a show built around Royce versus Sakuraba. Fans of MMA at the Dome and across the world weren't disappointed, as the fight lived up to every possible expectation anyone could have had for it. It went down as what many people consider to be the greatest mixed martial arts bout in history.

Royce had made a few demands for the fight. There would be no time limit, and the only way to win would be by knockout, submission, or if the fighter's corner threw in the towel. The referee would not be allowed to stop the fight, and since there was no time limit, there would be no ringside judges for the bout. The fight would be broken down into fifteen-minute rounds. All of this meant that the fight would keep going until one fighter couldn't take any more.

And that's exactly what happened, as Royce and Sakuraba battled for an unbelievable ninety minutes. Any mixed martial artist will tell you that the amount of energy expended in just a fifteen-minute fight is incredible, and it's extremely difficult to go that length of time, let alone ninety minutes, or six fifteen-minute rounds. No fight in MMA history, before or since, has come close to that length and still remained an exciting bout.

The first two fifteen-minute rounds saw Royce do very well against Sakuraba, although Sakuraba nearly got a kneebar on Royce at the end of the first round. After those initial two rounds, the fight continued for four more very exciting rounds until, in the sixth round, Sakuraba started to seriously damage Royce with leg kicks, and Royce tired out. After the sixth round ended, Royce's corner threw in the towel, giving Sakuraba the legendary win. It took ninety minutes of nonstop action to exhaust Royce. Sakuraba never got tired (after this fight, he even continued in the night's tournament, putting up a valiant effort to nearly defeat the much larger and very highly skilled Igor Vovchanchyn). This marathon match truly represented the pinnacle of what could be accomplished between two premier athletes in MMA.

Although Royce had lost for the first time in his career under MMA rules, it took ninety minutes for his opponent to finish him, and instead of taking away from Royce's legend, the bout just added to it. Royce, despite his small physical size, again increased his larger-than-life stature in the world of martial arts.

"We will probably never see a match like this again in terms of symbolism and overtones, not to mention that it lasted ninety minutes!" recalls Quadros, who did the play-by-play for the American home video release of the match.

Royce again took some time off from MMA, making it clear to any interested parties that he was only willing to fight once in a while at this point in his career, and that he would only fight when certain rules and conditions for his fights were met.

In his first fight following his loss to Sakuraba, controversy arose surrounding the rules that Royce demanded for his fights. Hidehiko Yoshida was a gold medalist in judo at the '92 Olympics in Barcelona, and a national sports hero in Japan. In the summer of 2002, he had signed a contract with PRIDE to make his debut in mixed martial arts with their promotion at a stadium show they were planning for August of that year. Yoshida would be Royce's first opponent since he fought Sakuraba over two years earlier.

The August 2002 show took place at Tokyo National Stadium, headlined by an all-star lineup of fights, and drawing a crowd of 71,000 fans paying $7 million U.S.—a record gate in the worlds of both mixed martial arts and pro wrestling across the entire globe. Royce Gracie versus Hidehiko Yoshida was an interesting matchup, as Yoshida was one of the best judoka in recent times, and the same can be said of Royce in Brazilian Jiu Jitsu. Judo versus jiu jitsu is a feud that dates back decades, and this fight would be another chapter in both of these martial arts' legacies. MMA had evolved considerably since Royce fought Sakuraba, and no one could tell how Royce would fare following his two-year hiatus from the sport.

The rules for the Yoshida-Royce confrontation were similar to those for Royce's fight with Sakuraba. The biggest difference was that, instead of having no time limit, the fight would take place in two ten-minute rounds, and if there was no winner in that span of time, the fight would be declared a draw, instead of it going to the judges for a decision.

In one of the more controversial finishes in MMA history, Yoshida, who for the most part had been winning the fight up to that point, appeared to have nearly caught Royce in a choke while lying on top of him on the ground. Although it was against the rules for the referee to stop the bout under any circumstances, the ref did so anyways just after the seven-minute mark, feeling that Royce had been defeated.

Yoshida was the victor, and the people of Japan were happy because of his sports-hero status. But Royce was angry. Although Yoshida had been dominating up to that point in the bout, and although there's a strong chance that Yoshida would have been able to finish him before the end of the round, many felt that Royce was unfairly cheated out of the match since it was simply against the rules for the ref to stop the bout. Furthermore, the instant replay of the finish showed that Royce did not seem to be choked out yet when the fight was stopped, although there was a very good chance that Yoshida was going to be able to choke Royce at any moment, given the position they were in on the ground.

Royce wanted a rematch, but he would have to wait until New Year's Eve 2003 for it to happen. "The first time Yoshida and I fought, the fight was unfairly stopped, and it left a very sick feeling in me," said Royce in an interview with *Pride FC*. "I was disgusted with MMA in general. If such a thing can happen to me, it can happen to any fighter at any time. For the past year, my management and PRIDE have been trying to set things right, and PRIDE came through; they offered a rematch with Yoshida, and I accepted on the spot."

On December 31, 2003, nearly sixteen months after that first controversial encounter between Royce and Yoshida, the MMA world was rocked when three mixed martial arts companies put on shows in Japan—all in huge stadiums, all on the same night, all at exactly the same time—in the ultimate promotional war. Antonio Inoki, founder of New Japan Pro Wrestling (which was unsuccessfully trying to branch out into MMA), ran a show at Kobe Wing Stadium headlined by pro wrestler Kazuyuki Fujita against boxer Imamu Mayfield. K-1, the world's biggest kickboxing company and one of the major sports franchises in Japan, held a show at the Nagoya Dome headlined by the record-breaking Bob Sapp against sumo legend Akebono. And, in front of 35,000 people, Royce Gracie once again took on Hidehiko Yoshida in the main event of PRIDE's show at the Saitama Super Arena.

Yoshida had certain problems going into the fight this time around. He had competed in the brutal two-night PRIDE Middleweight Grand Prix tournament earlier in 2003, and had sustained many damaging injuries in his bouts with Kiyoshi Tamura and Wanderlei Silva. The last night of the tournament was in November, just weeks before Yoshida's New Year's Eve fight against Royce, so Yoshida didn't have time to rest and heal his wounds, nor was he able to train. Yoshida went into the rematch out of shape.

Royce went into it in perfect shape, with the perfect strategy, and a perfect mind-set. Royce badly wanted this fight to prove to the world that their first bout should not have ended as it did, and this desire fueled the fire within him that he would use to light up Yoshida in their New Year's Eve main event.

Unexpectedly, Royce removed his gi, which he always wore, before the fight, in a strategy to throw Yoshida off, since the gi is very important in both jiu jitsu and judo. Yoshida did well in the fight at first, but Royce's great conditioning overcame Yoshida's lack of conditioning, and Royce, a much smaller man than Yoshida, managed to handle the judo master throughout the second round.

Royce had demanded that the fight be held under similar rules to their first: no judges, the ref can't stop the fight, the only way to lose is by submission or if your corner throws in the towel, and the match lasts for two ten-minute rounds. Royce also demanded a non-Japanese referee, since he felt that the Japanese referee had screwed him in his last bout against Yoshida, so PRIDE judge Matt Hume was selected as ref.

The fact that Royce requested all of these rules and stipulations is ironic, since he dominated the fight and clearly would have won a decision had he allowed judges to be ringside for the bout. But after embarrassing Yoshida and not so much proving himself to the world as proving what a smaller man with great conditioning can do to a bigger man with no conditioning, Royce had to settle for the moral victory. "I came to the fight to win, and I did everything to get there," said Royce in a post-fight interview with *Pride FC*. "The fight was officially a draw, and I am not changing that at all, but watch the fight, and you tell me who is the winner."

Of course, this wasn't the last fight for Royce Gracie, as he returned to the ring exactly one year later to be a part of the 2004 New Year's Eve extravaganza in Japan. But this time it wasn't for PRIDE, as Royce had signed a deal with K-1 and was scheduled to fight sumo Akebono, who remains one of the biggest sports stars in Japan today.

Of course, sumos have very little chance against a skilled mixed martial artist, and this fight was simply a freak show to draw TV ratings in Japan, where people would tune in to see the miniscule Royce defeat the behemoth Akebono. And submitting Akebono quickly, that's exactly what he did.

CONCLUSION

To ask someone to select the single greatest fighter in UFC history is impossible. It's a question with no answer. The objective of this book was to look at the field of fighters who have had lengthy careers in the UFC, and to present a ranking of fighters who might *possibly* be considered the greatest in UFC history, then to allow readers to draw their own conclusions based on the merits of each fighter.

Determining the greatest fighter in UFC history (or PRIDE history, or K-1 history, or even complete mixed martial arts history) is a lot like trying to determine the greatest singer in history. There are no real credentials that a singer could have that would make her or him the best in history, period. You might look at who has the most gold records, but that would create a list of the *best-selling* singers in history, not necessarily the "greatest." You could try to determine who is the most talented, possibly by looking at the critical acclaim for their work, but with such a method, you'd simply be forming an opinion based on the opinions of others.

Just as there is no single greatest singer in history, there is no single greatest mixed martial artist in UFC history. That's why the subject of this book is an oxymoron; it really shouldn't exist, because it's an attempt to come up with a definitive answer to a rhetorical question.

Royce Gracie was an easy selection for the greatest fighter in UFC history because of his influence on the sport and his success in the promotion in the early '90s, as well as for all of the other reasons outlined in his biography earlier in this book. I also believe the second and third choices—Ken and Frank Shamrock, respectively—were easy to rank.

I can understand an argument for Ken Shamrock as the greatest fighter in UFC history, but not for Frank (I'll get to that in a moment). In terms of marketing, Ken Shamrock represented the pinnacle of what UFC could become in the '90s; he was the quintessential mixed martial artist, without even having to actually be the best fighter. At the time of the UFC's run of greatest popularity in the '90s, Ken was the fighter whom a lot of people were willing to pay a lot of money to see. He was the money draw, and even in reality fighting, illusion often means more than reality.

The main reason I selected Royce Gracie for the number-one spot in this ranking is that, equally influential and as much a money draw as Ken, he had a higher success rate throughout the 1990s. Royce Gracie is the most influential mixed martial artist in history, and he'll remain that way forever, because everything that has followed him in MMA is, in part, a reference back to him. You can't have someone more influential than the guy who started it all in the octagon.

The reason that Frank Shamrock could never be considered the greatest mixed martial artist on any list is that, although his résumé is very complete, when you look at all of his attributes, he's bested by at least one other fighter in every category. Frank was incredibly influential, but not to the degree that Royce was. Pound for pound, Frank was the best fighter on the planet in the late '90s, but he wouldn't rank anywhere near that level today because the MMA world has caught up to—and even surpassed—him. He was a money draw for UFC when the company was in shambles, which means that every money draw before him, and after him, actually most likely drew more money. Frank Shamrock will always exist as the right guy at the wrong time. If he had come along three years earlier or three years later, he'd be far more qualified for the top spot on this list. Timing is everything.

From there, I think the ranking of the rest of the fighters, and who actually makes the list, is a matter of perspective. In my opinion, anyone who argues about where Don Frye, Tito Ortiz, Dan Severn, or whoever else should be ranked—whether they should be number five, or six, or seven—is completely missing the point. I think that the only valid argument is for who should be on the list, in no particular order, and who should be dropped.

My opinion is that the biggest controversy that this book will create is the ranking of Tank Abbott as number ten, which will probably make more than one person who doesn't bother to read this book laugh. I know Tank Abbott is not a money draw. I know Tank Abbott hasn't won a fight since 1998. But Tank Abbott has been extremely influential over the course of UFC history based on what he did (or, technically, didn't) do, and the way he was promoted by SEG. But believe me, it's no mistake that Tank was in the last spot on the list.

With the success of *The Ultimate Fighter* on Spike TV in early 2005, I believe UFC is climbing to a new level of popularity that may very well surpass its mid-1990s popularity. I believe this resurgence will completely change this "top-ten" list since, as mixed martial arts continues to grow in North America, new fighters will need to be added, and some of the current fighters will need to be dropped.

If Randy Couture continues to become more popular—not so much in mixed martial arts, where he is already popular enough, but outside of the sport—to the degree that the casual public recognizes him as a celebrity, and as long as he continues to win at a high level and his age doesn't catch up to him in the next couple of years, he could very well end up the greatest fighter in UFC history. This would be based on a combination of his celebrity value, his money-drawing appeal, and his incredible skill and success as a fighter. But he doesn't have much time left, and it's left to wonder what would have become of him had the UFC existed when he was twenty-five.

In summary, this book is a tribute to the fighters who established the UFC and made mixed martial arts what it is in North America today, and what it will continue to be tomorrow and beyond. Every single fighter profiled in this book was influential in the course of mixed martial arts history, some in more ways than one. Each is part of the building blocks on which the industry stands today, and that is why I consider them the greatest fighters in UFC history.

SOURCES

A note on interviews: All interviews conducted by the author took place between January and May 2004, with the exception of the Dan Severn interview, which took place in October 2003.

Boone, Matt, and John Hartnett. "Tank Abbott Interview." *WrestleZone Radio.* http://www.mmanews.com/ufc/interviews/tankabbott/index.shtml. 2004.

Boxing Insider. "Interview with 'The Huntington Beach Bad Boy' Tito Ortiz." *Wrestlingdotcom.* http://www.wrestlingdotcom.com/news/81949804.php?vo=69. 22 March 2004.

—. "Interview with UFC Legend Tank Abbott." 14 Nov. 2003. http://www.boxinginsider.com/mma/stories/70881611.php. 2004.

Coleman, Mark. Phone interview with author. 2004.

Couture, Randy. Phone interview with author. 2004.

"Frank Juarez Shamrock's Bio." 2002. Frank Shamrock Official Website. http://www.frankshamrock.org/default.asp?pg=16. 2004.

Frye, Don. Phone interview with author. 2004.

Gentry, Clyde. *No Holds Barred: Evolution.* Texas: Archon Publishing, 2000.

Gracie Academy press release, 1998.

Krauss, Erich, and Bret Aita. *Brawl: A Behind-the-Scenes Look at Mixed Martial Arts Competition.* Toronto: ECW Press, 2002.

Martial Arts Gazette [on-line]. Interview with Royce Gracie. http://www.roycegracie.tv/fan/interview/8.htm.

McCarthy, John. E-mail to author. 2004.

Meltzer, Dave. E-mail to author. 2004.

—. Phone interview with author. 2004.

MMA Weekly Radio. "Interview: Tito Ortiz." http://www.mmaweekly.com/interviews/iv_TitoOrtiz-03-30-04.html. 30 March 2004.

Osborne, Jeff. Phone interview with author. 2004.

Pooch. "UFC Middleweight Champion Tito Ortiz Interview Part 1." *SFUK.* 2 Oct. 2001. http://sfuk.tripod.com/interviews_01/tito_interview1.html. 2004.

Pride FC. Interview with Ken Shamrock. http://www.pridefc.com/interviews/shamrock_01/shamrock.htm. 2004.

—. "Interview with Mark Coleman." 24 April 2004. http://www.pridefc.com/ interviews/coleman_02/coleman_02.htm. 2004.

—. Don Frye interview. http://www.pridefc.com/interviews/frye_04/frye.htm. 2003.

—. Interview with Royce Gracie. http://www.roycegracie.tv/news/ 112804/ interview_pride.htm. 2004.

Quadros, Stephen. E-mail to author. 2004.

—. Phone interview with author. 2004.

Severn, Dan. Phone interview with author. 2003.

Shamrock, Frank. Phone interview with author. 2004.

Shamrock, Ken. Phone interview with author. 2004.

Sherdog.com. "Mark 'The Hammer' Coleman Interview." 18 December 2000. http://www.sherdog.com/interviews/coleman/coleman1.shtm. 2004.

—. "Don Frye Interview, 13 August 2000." http://www.sherdog.com/interviews/ frye/fryeinterview.shtm. 2004.

—. "Maurice Smith Interview, 8 Nov. 2000." http://www.sherdog.com/interviews/maurice smith/mosmithinterview1.shtm. 2004.

—. "Interview with Tank Abbott." 2001. http://www.onzuka.com/news_2001July3.html. 2004.

Shickell, Matt. Randy Couture interview. *SFUK.* http://sfuk.tripod.com/interviews_04/randy_ couture.html. April 2004.

Sloan, Mike. "Interview with Frank Shamrock." 2002. Sherdog.com http://www.sherdog.com. 2004.

—. "Interview: Tito Ortiz!" *UFCFightNews.* 2001. http://www.ufcfightnews.com/ news/titoortiz3.html. 2004.

Smith, Maurice. Phone interview with author. 2004.

Ultimate Royce Gracie. UFC Home Video. Zuffa, LLC, 2003.

WR. "An Interview with Frank Shamrock." *Real Fighting.* http://www.realfighting.com/ 0102/shamint.htm. 2004.